EVERYDAY WRITING

EveryDay Writing

FOR FUN, FOR PROFIT,

FOR YOUR HEART'S CONTENT

Laurie Rozakis, Ph.D.

MADISON
PARK
PRESS™

NEW YORK

Published by Madison Park Press, 15 East 26th Street, New York, NY 10010. Madison Park Press is a trademark of Bookspan.

Book design by Christos Peterson

ISBN: 978-1-58288-279-6

Printed in the United States of America

To SGK: dear friend, loyal friend, best friend.
From producing a crowbar in April 1973 to
photographing a wedding in October 2007,
you're always there for us.

(And I still owe you thanks for your help
with *The Portable Jewish Mother.*)
—LNR

Contents

⟶ ∽∾∿ ⟵

CHAPTER 1
You *Can* Be a Creative Writer

———⊶⊷———

On the surface, Charles Lutwidge Dodgson certainly didn't seem to have what it takes to be a creative writer. First of all, he made his living as a mathematician and logician . . . and we all know that math people aren't creative. They spend their days crunching numbers. How creative is *that*?

Cheaper by the Dozen?
Second, Charles was largely homeschooled. Born in 1832, he was one of eleven children—seven girls and four boys—so how could he get much attention from his parents? His father was a minister, which meant that the family was hardly wealthy. When Charles was a teenager, he went to a boarding school, but he was miserable there. Fortunately, he was much happier in college, but things didn't go as well as he would have liked. He failed an important scholarship test because he didn't work hard enough, which he admitted. How could an intelligent but lazy student have the ambition to succeed as a creative writer?

Third, Charles had a severe stammer that made him so self-conscious that he abandoned his first career goal: he had wanted to follow in his father's footsteps and become a minister. He was also almost completely deaf in his right ear and suffered from frequent upper respiratory infections as a result of a severe bout of whooping cough. How could a partially handicapped man succeed as a creative writer?

Never Give Up

But none of these challenges discouraged Charles from trying to become a creative writer. From his childhood, he wrote poetry and short stories and even sent them off to magazines. Some were actually published! During the time he was twenty-two to twenty-four years old, Charles's work appeared in many well-known British magazines, some focusing on humor, one of his special interests. Charles may have been lazy when it came to his schoolwork, but he wasn't slothful when it came to his creative writing. He was also quite ambitious. In 1855, he wrote to a friend, "I do not think I have yet written anything worthy of real publication, but I do not despair of doing so someday."

Charles firmly believed that anyone could become a creative writer through desire, determination, and practice. He believed that a creative writer is made, not born, and that anyone who worked hard enough at the craft of writing could make it. Charles even wrote a poem about his quest to become a successful creative writer. I know you'll enjoy his humor and jabs at people who give advice to those wanting to express their creativity in writing. Here is Charles's poem. As you read it, notice the advice he has been given by his grandfather.

Poeta Fit, Non Nascitur (A Poet Is Made, Not Born)

"How shall I be a poet?
How shall I write in rhyme?
You told me once 'the very wish
Partook of the sublime.'
Then tell me how! Don't put me off
With your 'another time'!"

The old man smiled to see him,
To hear his sudden sally;
He liked the lad to speak his mind
Enthusiastically;
And thought "There's no hum-drum in him,
Nor any shilly-shally."

"And would you be a poet
Before you've been to school?
Ah, well! I hardly thought you
So absolute a fool.
First learn to be spasmodic—
A very simple rule.

"For first you write a sentence,
And then you chop it small;
Then mix the bits, and sort them out
Just as they chance to fall:
The order of the phrases makes
No difference at all.

"Then, if you'd be impressive,
Remember what I say,
That abstract qualities begin
With capitals always:
The True, the Good, the Beautiful—
Those are the things that pay!

"Next, when we are describing
A shape, or sound, or tint;
Don't state the matter plainly,
But put it in a hint;
And learn to look at all things
With a sort of mental squint."

"For instance, if I wished, Sir,
Of mutton-pies to tell,
Should I say 'dreams of fleecy flocks
Pent in a wheaten cell'?"
"Why, yes," the old man said: "that phrase
Would answer very well."

"Then fourthly, there are epithets
That suit with any word—
As well as Harvey's Reading Sauce
With fish, or flesh, or bird—

Of these, 'wild,' 'lonely,' 'weary,' 'strange,'
Are much to be preferred."

"And will it do, O will it do
To take them in a lump—
As 'the wild man went his weary way
To a strange and lonely pump'?"
"Nay, nay! You must not hastily
To such conclusions jump.

"Such epithets, like pepper,
Give zest to what you write;
And, if you strew them sparely,
They whet the appetite:
But if you lay them on too thick,
You spoil the matter quite!

"Last, as to the arrangement:
Your reader, you should show him,
Must take what information he
Can get, and look for no im
mature disclosure of the drift
And purpose of your poem.

"Therefore to test his patience—
How much he can endure—
Mention no places, names, or dates,
And evermore be sure
Throughout the poem to be found
Consistently obscure.

. . . .

"Now try your hand, ere Fancy
Have lost its present glow—"
"And then," his grandson added,
"We'll publish it, you know:
Green cloth—gold-lettered at the back—
In duodecimo!" [A book format]

Then proudly smiled that old man
To see the eager lad
Rush madly for his pen and ink
And for his blotting-pad—
But, when he thought of publishing,
His face grew stern and sad.

A Creative Writer Is Made, Not Born

I agree with what Charles wrote in his poem. Specifically, I believe that

❧ You don't need to have emotional hissy fits when you write. Much of creative writing is based on emotion, but it can be emotion recollected in tranquility, as William Wordsworth said. You don't have to tear out your hair, toss and turn all night, or bite your nails to the quick to become a fine creative writer.

❧ You don't want to chop your sentences into small bits and let the words stay where they fall. Instead, you will construct your sentences carefully to convey a specific meaning and feeling.

❧ You won't capitalize Random Nouns to sound impressive and stuffy. Instead, you will follow the rules of standard written English. (And not to worry—I've included a review of style and grammar that's simple and easy to understand.)

❧ You won't make your reader hunt for meaning. Instead, you will write clearly and directly, choosing specific and precise words to communicate your ideas to your audience.

❧ You won't use clichéd descriptions such as *wild, lonely, weary,* and *strange.* Instead, you will find fresh and exciting ways to express your meaning. You will help your readers see the world in new ways.

❧ You'll never get upset about publishing. There are so many ways to publish today—traditional ways such as print books and exciting new ways such as blogs and Web pages—that you will be able to publish your creative writing if you decide that you want to share it.

And most of all, I believe that anyone who wants to become a successful creative writer can make his or her dream come true. In the pages ahead, I'll get you started on the path to expressing your imagination in words.

A Surprise Ending

Oh, by the way, what ever happened to Charles? Did he become a creative writer? Did he achieve his dream? He sure did: not only did he write what he wanted, but in so doing, he also became one of the most successful creative writers of the twentieth century. I'll bet you've heard of at least one of his books and have probably read it, too. But you don't know him as Charles Lutwidge Dodgson; you know him under his pen name: Lewis Carroll. His *Alice's Adventures in Wonderland* was published in 1865 and *Through the Looking Glass,* in 1872. He also wrote the wonderfully creative nonsense poem *The Hunting of the Snark* (1876) and many more.

> Charles Lutwidge Dodgson lived from 1832 to 1898. In addition to being a renowned writer of children's books, poetry, and mathematical treatises, he also achieved fame as a photographer.

Finding Your Destiny Through Creative Writing

Like all creative writers, Charles Dodgson wrote because he loved it. He wrote because it filled his soul with joy, as it does yours and mine. He wrote because it made him feel fulfilled, because he had a message to pass on, because it was something he felt compelled to do. He wrote because creative writing nourishes the soul as few other artistic undertakings can. The American writer Truman Capote put it this way: "To me, the greatest pleasure of writing is not what it's about, but the inner music that words make."

That's because creative writing allows you to

assert your demands	boost your creativity
cement a friendship	communicate your ideas
channel your emotions	cope with traumatic loss
declare your love	display your inventiveness
entertain others	evaluate something
express your feelings	explore an idea
explore yourself	find solace in a confusing world
free yourself from inhibitions	interpret information
inspire others to create	make a difference in the world
move others to action or belief	travel the road to self-discovery
pledge your support	promote self-understanding
raise your self-esteem	report information
record a memory	wash away bitterness
settle disputes, even wars!	share your artistry
stretch the boundaries of the form	tap into the well-spring of your energy
vent your frustrations	work through anger and despair

Creative writing is self-expression, liberation from the constraints of everyday life. And when you write, you are strong. Modern writer John Updike compares being a creative writer to being a sailor who sets a course out to sea. A creative writer is like an explorer, a groundbreaker.

There are many different *ways* people write, just as there are many different reasons *why* they write. Later in this book we'll explore the ways—the methods of writing—so you can find the ones that best suit your audience and style. Right now, let me prove that you can be a creative writer. How can I be so sure? It's easy: because so many other people just like you have been smashing successes. (And I'm one of them!)

You Can Have a Completely Different Day Job

Erle Stanley Gardner, the author of more than eighty Perry Mason novels, was a lawyer. So are John Grisham and Scott Turow, to mention just the most famous ones. Many successful creative writers have been doctors, including thriller writers

Michael Crichton and Robin Cook, Russian playwright Anton Chekhov, Sherlock Holmes creator Sir Arthur Conan Doyle, self-help guru Deepak Chopra, and *Joy of Sex* author Alex Comfort. Doctor, lawyer, Indian chief; tinker, tailor, soldier, spy—no matter what you do, you can be a creative writer as well.

You Can Keep Your Identity Secret

You have read that Charles Dodgson wrote under the pen name Lewis Carroll. Writers have many different reasons for concealing their identities. Some, such as Emily Brontë, knew that in their day they would never be published if people knew they were women. Others, like Stephen King, take a pen name for some of their work because they have such a prodigious output that they fear they'll flood the market with their writing. Still others, such as William Sidney Porter, are hiding a shameful past. Porter took the pen name O. Henry after he was convicted and jailed for bank robbery.

And some just want to have fun, so they take more imaginative pen names: Charles Farrar Browne took the pen name Artemus Ward, Joel Chandler Harris took the pen name Uncle Remus, and Robert Henry Newell took the pen name Orpheus C. Kerr. If you don't want people to know that you're trying to become a creative writer, you can simply take a pen name.

You Don't Even Need Much Time

Some writers labor for decades and produce few books, but superb ones. Ralph Ellison, author of *Invisible Man*, and Joseph Heller, author of *Catch-22*, are cases in point. But other writers produce good—even great—creative writing very quickly, so don't despair if you don't have much time. Let me prove to you that you always have enough time to write:

- 🕒 Anne Rice wrote *Interview with a Vampire* (1977) in five weeks in order to meet a contest deadline. (She didn't win the prize, but the novel did become a best seller.)

- 🕒 Louisa May Alcott wrote *Little Women* (1871) in three weeks while she was on vacation in Rome. She wrote *Eight Cousins* (1874) in six weeks. So take a vacation and write a book!

❧ Daniel Defoe is most famous for *The Life and Strange Surprising Adventures of Robinson Crusoe*. The book was so popular that he wrote the sequel, *The Further Adventures of Robinson Crusoe,* in a month.

❧ Erle Stanley Gardner wrote his first Perry Mason novel in three and a half days. He dictated it—and so can you.

❧ Honoré de Balzac wrote *Le Père Goriot* (1834) in one month and ten days. He wrote twenty-four hours a day, gulping down strong coffee. I don't recommend this method.

So Let's Get Started!

There's no time like the present, so why not reward yourself with a little writing fun? Make a cup of coffee, sharpen your pencil or turn on the computer, and let your creativity emerge. Choose one of the following story starters to complete.

❧ She gazed out of the airplane window as the plane descended for a landing. But she didn't see the tiny cars racing down the freeway or the whitecaps on the ocean, because she was preoccupied. What would it be like now? Would she still adore it, after all these years? Glancing at her cell phone, she realized with a shock that in a few moments she would come face-to-face with her past.

❧ The air felt strangely still, the absence of noise disquieting.

"Lucy, can you see it?" Mark asked.

"See what? Mark, you're scaring me." Lucy's eyes strained to make out the shadows in the dim light outside the hall window.

"Focus, honey. Just focus on the empty lot next door," Mark begged.

"I can see the old chain-link fence," Lucy said. "What else do you want me to see?" she asked.

"The mountain. It wasn't there before," Mark responded.

"Don't be an idiot. Mountains don't rise up in ten minutes," Lucy said in a quavering voice.

"When we looked out a few minutes ago, we could see the apartment building and the movie theater in the village. Where are they now?" Mark asked.

"They're . . . they're . . . oh . . ." Lucy trailed off.

You Must Remember This

You *can* be a creative writer. You have the ability and the desire. You just need determination, so stick with it.

$\mathcal{C}$HAPTER 2
What Motivates *You* to Become a Creative Writer?

> I celebrate myself, and sing myself,
> And what I assume you shall assume,
> For every atom belonging to me as good belongs to you.
>
> I loafe and invite my soul,
> I lean and loafe at my ease observing a spear of summer grass.
>
> —Walt Whitman, "Song of Myself"

Creative writing is singing a song of self, as Whitman did so famously more than a century ago. It's not egotism or arrogance. Rather, it's a heartfelt sharing of who you are and what you value. The reasons why people suddenly decide to take the plunge and write creatively are as varied and special as people themselves. Why did *you* decide to start writing? See which of the following reasons most closely match your own emotions. Perhaps you'll discover that you have even more reasons for becoming a creative writer than you thought.

> Walt Whitman didn't hesitate to write creatively. Some people reacted with horror, but many others embraced the often shocking poet and essayist. Not only did he write about himself, but he also threw out the standard rules of poetry to embrace *free verse*, poetry without a regular pattern of rhyme. He used this new type of writing to convey his idea that America was certain to be the country to free the human spirit. He was right, wasn't he?

Write Creatively for Self-Discovery

Creative writing allows you to think about things aloud, to find out more about yourself. Sometimes it's not until you've put thoughts into words that you're able to understand how you really feel. The act of articulating your ideas gives them substance.

I was tossing this idea around with my friend Betty Gold, one of the smartest people I know. She had asked me what a certain tree in my yard was called. I responded, "I don't know. It's just a tree." She replied, "If you can't name it precisely, you don't know it." Her comment resonated with me because I realized that she was correct. Writing creatively helps us name ideas and things, making the abstract into the concrete.

Below is part of a contemporary blog. As you read, decide why the author wrote the entry.

Well, 2007 is finally here! This will be a year of studying abroad, finishing college, going to graduate school, figuring out what to do with my life . . . totally an important year.

I've actually decided to write some resolutions this year. Here they are:

—I will ask for help when I need it.

—I will have more fun!

—I will tell people what I'm really thinking instead of keeping it inside and letting it rattle around.

—I will focus on things that are really important to me.

—I will go on more road trips to see awesome people.

—I will wear my sunshine yellow crocs to graduation.

—I will take pictures (that's not that hard for me, as most of you know).

—I will relax more.

Just a few that came into my head. I hope everyone has a safe and happy New Year.

Creative writing is so flexible that it encourages writers to experiment with form, strategy, and approaches. You can pick a writing pattern that has worked for you in the past, or try an entirely new one. This is implied in one of the words we use for a common writing form: the *essay*. The word *essay* comes from the French word *essayer*, which means "to try." You'll learn more about essays in chapter 7.

As you write, you're trying to find new avenues to explore, new things to discover. By providing an opportunity for testing new ideas instead of proving concepts that are already accepted, creative writing can reveal measureless new vistas.

When you write to understand more about yourself, you can make the most of your talents and opportunities. As you write for self-discovery, try these suggestions:

- ❧ Start by looking inside yourself and probing your feelings, as the writer of the blog did. As you write, you can ask yourself such questions as "How do I feel?" "What makes me feel this way?" "Why did I take this action?" and "How will I feel about this action in the future?"

- ❧ Or you might try to make discoveries about yourself by looking through the eyes of others. In this case, ask yourself such questions as "How have my parents shaped me?" "How did this experience help me do something I might not ordinarily have done?"

- ❧ You might also look for parallels between what you see in the world around you and how you perceive yourself. You can contrast your father's or mother's character to your own, for instance, or consider how the cycles of nature affect your behavior.

You may have been using writing as a voyage of creative self-discovery for quite some time—or you may have decided that the unexamined life *is* indeed worth living. It's natural for us to swing from one extreme to the other as we mature.

Write Creatively to Reach Out to Others
Writing is probably the most powerful way we have to communicate because unlike speech or sex, it's lasting. A spoken word vanishes into the air; a written word stays imprinted on the page. And let's not talk about sex . . .

That's why creative writing helps us communicate with others. It also helps eliminate possible misunderstandings because you can carefully craft what you want to say. The following blog entry asks readers for advice. How would you answer this writer?

My father always had a lot of hair. He didn't start losing it until he was well into his fifties, and then it only receded a little in the front. My maternal grandfather, on the other hand, was bald by the time he was 30.

Guess who I take after? Hmmm.

I had always heard that male-pattern baldness comes from the maternal side, but I never believed it. It's surely true where my pate is concerned. My hair is receding at an alarming rate. I am definitely starting to look more and more like Gramps at my age.

So the question is: Do I start taking anti-hair loss pills and applying anti-hair loss liquids or do I just surrender to the inevitable? Maybe I should short-circuit the entire process and just shave my head. That looks sorta cool nowadays. I'm open for suggestions, people.

Write Creatively to Express Your Feelings

Think about writing to reach out to others. Why do you need people? Well, often you just need to blow off some steam. You don't want or need feedback, so you don't necessarily want to talk to someone. Creative writing is a perfect way to express minor annoyances. The following blog shows how one person used creative writing this way. How often would you like to release your feelings this way?

I like to watch the local news in the morning. Is this so much to ask? I guess so, because today the TV didn't work. I called the cable provider. Easy, eh? Yeah, until I was on hold for 39 minutes. Listening to their annoying commercials . . . over and over and over. I was *finally* connected to a technician and the problem was fixed in 10 minutes. So nearly an hour wasted on a problem caused by the cable provider.

Then I went to the drug store. The people who work there are all stupid! I just went to pick up my medicine and I had to tell them my name, address, etc., just to make sure it is really me. Then I bought paper towels on sale for $2.79 and some other things. I also had to return something I didn't need. Well, the girl behind the register tells me that I didn't pay for it with my Amex card; I must have used ANOTHER one! I told her I have only one credit card. Of course I had used my Amex. I finally figured out that the 4 digits shown on my receipt don't correspond with the actual #s on the card because of the way the card is swiped. Then I get home, I look at my receipt and see that they charged me $3.99 for each 4-pack of paper towels instead of the $2.97. ARRRGGHH!!!

Mary Huestis Pengilly became homeless as a result of the Saint John, New Brunswick, fire of 1877. She wrote her book, *Diary Written in the Provincial Lunatic Asylum*, not only to heal her pain but also to reveal the inner workings of the asylums of the time and to prompt officials to find better methods to help the homeless and mentally ill.

Write Creatively for Healing

We all carry some excess baggage. Sometimes those bags get a little too heavy and a personal crisis erupts. This is a lot different from mere venting; in these instances, you're in real personal distress. You can pay a therapist to listen, talk to a friend, press on doggedly—or write about your feelings. Creative writing is one of the best ways to deal with an upsetting personal issue. In fact, the beneficial effects of creative writing have been documented in many rigorous scientific studies. People of all ages feel better after writing about upsetting feelings, memories, and events.

Even more amazing, the beneficial effect of creative writing is physical as well as emotional. A study published in the *Journal of Consulting and Clinical Psychology* found that students had more T-lymphocyte cells after writing about upsetting events. T-lymphocyte cells indicate a healthy immune system. A 1999 medical study found that creative writing can even help relieve the symptoms of various medical conditions, including asthma and rheumatoid arthritis. Doctors can't explain these results, but many doctors believe that creative writing helps relieve stress. We know that stress worsens many diseases by weakening the immune system.

How can creative writing relieve stress? Writing about your feelings helps you understand them. This leads to a sense of control. When you're in control, you can better manage stressful and upsetting events.

In what ways do you think writing the diary entry below might have helped the author resolve some key issues in her life? Mary Huestis Pengilly wrote this entry while she was a patient in 1885 in the Provincial Lunatic Asylum in New Brunswick, Canada.

December—They will not allow me to go home, and I must write these things down for fear I forget. It will help to pass the time away. It is very hard to endure this prison life, and know that my sons think me insane when I am not. . . .

I can't bear to see myself in the glass, I am so wasted—so miserable. My poor boys, no wonder you look so sad, to see your mother looking so badly, and be compelled to leave her here alone among strangers who know nothing about her past life. They don't seem to have any respect for me. If I were the most miserable woman in the city of St. John, I would be entitled to better treatment at the hands of those who are paid by the Province to make us as comfortable as they can, by keeping us warmed and fed, as poor feeble invalids should be kept. Sometimes I almost sink in despair. One consolation is left me—some day death will unlock those prison doors, and my freed spirit will go forth rejoicing in its liberty.

I come back to my own room and write again; what shall I do? I cannot—how can I stay here any longer! and I cannot get away, locked in as prisoners in our rooms at night, fed like paupers. If I were committed to the penitentiary for a crime, I would not be used any worse than I am here. My heart longs for sympathy, and has it not.

Venting your emotions through writing carries a great bonus, too: as you heal, you often tap your hidden creativity. Later we'll look more deeply into this use of creative writing. I'll teach you some ways to make this method work for you.

> *Primary sources* are created by direct observation. The writers participated in the events being described. Primary sources include autobiographies, blogs, diaries, eyewitness events, interviews, and some historical documents. *Secondary sources*, in contrast, are reported after the fact. They are written by people with indirect knowledge. Secondary sources include abstracts, biographies, book reviews, encyclopedias, literary criticism, most newspaper and magazine articles, and most of the information in textbooks.

Write Creatively for Future Generations

Creative writing allows you to leave a legacy for the future. This can take the form of a journal, a diary, letters, or a book. It can be a printed blog, newspaper article, or poem, too. These so-called primary sources are invaluable historical records. Isn't it nice to think that by writing something today, you are leaving a historical record for generations to come?

Think about some events that have had a strong impact on you. Perhaps you've been touched by global events such as a war. Maybe the events are more private, such as personal accomplishments or family transitions. Cyrus Pringle, a Quaker, wrote the following diary entry in 1863. Pringle describes his experiences being a conscientious objector during the Civil War. What purpose do you think his account serves for contemporary readers?

> *Through the heat of this long ride, we felt our total lack of water and the meagerness of our supply of food. Our thirst became so oppressive as we were marched here from Culpeper, some four miles with scarcely a halt to rest, under our heavy loads, and through the heat and deep dust of the road, that we drank water and dipped in the brooks we passed, though it was discolored with the soap the soldiers had used in washing. The guns interfered with our walking, and, slipping down, dragged with painful*

weight upon our shoulders. Poor P.D. fell out from exhaustion and did not come in till we had been some little time at the camp. We were taken to the 4th Vermont regiment and soon apportioned to companies. Though we waited upon the officer commanding the company in which we were placed, and endeavored to explain our situation, we were required immediately after to be present at inspection of arms. We declined, but an attempt was made to force us to obedience, first, by the officers of the company, then, by those of the regiment; but, failing to exact obedience of us, we were ordered by the colonel to be tied, and, if we made outcry, to be gagged also, and to be kept so till he gave orders for our release. After two or three hours we were relieved and left under guard; lying down on the ground in the open air, and covering ourselves with our blankets, we soon fell asleep from exhaustion, and the fatigue of the day.

This morning the officers told us we must yield. We must obey and serve. We were threatened great severities and even death. We seem perfectly at the mercy of the military power, and, more, in the hands of the inferior officers, who, from their being far removed from Washington, feel less restraint from those Regulations of the Army, which are for the protection of privates from personal abuse.

The Civil War was the bloodiest conflict in American history, resulting in more American casualties than any other war. Pringle may not have realized that he was *seeing* history and that his writing ended up *preserving* history, but that's just what happened.

Creative writing for the future can take many forms. Here are some of the most common ones:

autobiographies	journals
blogs (be sure to print them out!)	letters
	memoirs
books	newspaper and
diaries	magazine articles
e-mail (print these out too!)	postcards

Write Creatively to Evaluate Something

Life is full of choices, big and small. Creative writing can help us sift through the choices to make the best possible decisions. Below is an excerpt from Mark Twain's famous critical review of James Fenimore Cooper's *The Deerslayer*, the fifth novel in his Leatherstocking Tales series. Twain's advice to Cooper is great advice to any creative writer.

> *There are nineteen rules governing literary art in the domain of romantic fiction—some say twenty-two. In* Deerslayer, *Cooper violated eighteen of them. These eighteen require:*
>
> 1. *That a tale shall accomplish something and arrive some-where. But the* Deerslayer *tale accomplishes nothing and arrives in the air.*
> 2. *They require that the episodes of a tale shall be necessary parts of the tale, and shall help develop it. But as the* Deerslayer *tale is not a tale, and accomplished nothing and arrives nowhere, the episodes have no rightful place in the work, since there was nothing for them to develop.*
> 3. *They require that the personages in a tale shall be alive, except in the cases of corpses, and that the reader shall be able to tell the corpses from the others. But this detail has often been overlooked in the* Deerslayer *tale. . . .*
>
> *In addition to these large rules there are some little ones. These require that the author shall:*
> 12. *Say what he is proposing to say, not merely come near it.*
> 13. *Use the right word, not its second cousin.*
> 14. *Eschew surplus.*
> 15. *Not omit any necessary details.*
> 16. *Avoid slovenliness of form.*
> 17. *Use good grammar.*
> 18. *Employ a simple and straightforward style.*
>
> *Even these seven are coldly and persistently violated in the* Deerslayer *tale.*

Writing fair and balanced evaluations requires you to write precisely and creatively.

Write Creatively to Entertain Others

Here's the scene: it's a sultry summer night. You're sitting on the lawn swing with an iced tea and the following two poems. Read the poems. Then decide what made them entertaining.

Example One:

A single flow'r he sent me, since we met.
    All tenderly his messenger he chose;
Deep-hearted, pure, with scented dew still wet—
    One perfect rose.

I knew the language of the floweret;
    "My fragile leaves," it said, "his heart enclose."
Love long has taken for his amulet
    One perfect rose.

Why is it no one ever sent me yet
    One perfect limousine, do you suppose?
Ah no, it's always just my luck to get
    One perfect rose.
        —Dorothy Parker, "One Perfect Rose"

Example Two:

I pray the Lord my soul to take
If the tax collector hasn't got it before I wake.
    —Ogden Nash, "One from One Leaves Two," stanza 5

Creative writing that entertains is fun to write as well as fun to read. If you find joy in writing to entertain others, it will come from knowing that you brought them pleasure. It is a rare and wonderful piece of writing that can make us laugh out loud, but even sparking a smile can make you say, "I did a good job with that writing!" Using words to amuse other people is a wondrous gift to them.

In a larger sense, when you help readers laugh about their tragedies as well as their triumphs, you help them deal with all situations. By reminding people that we all endure tough times, you help them feel part of a larger community. Humor thus helps people deal with human imperfection.

Write Creatively for Fun

To me, the most important reason for writing creatively is *pleasure*. You get only one chance at this world, so after you're released from the slog of sitting in your cubicle from nine to five, why not do something you want, something just for yourself? For many people, creative writing is that special something that relieves the daily grind.

There's no doubt that creative writing, as with any type of writing, is darned hard work, but it's also a lot of fun. If it's not, you're better off poking yourself in the eye with a fork, right? Mark Twain (Samuel Langhorne Clemens) wrote to make a living, but he clearly derived a great deal of pleasure from his creativity. To support a local charity, Twain wrote and delivered a brief speech before an audience in Vienna on March 10, 1899. Below is an especially humorous excerpt. It shows the delight that writing brought to Twain.

> *I have not sufficiently mastered German, to allow my using it with impunity. My collection of fourteen-syllable German words is still incomplete. But I have just added to that collection a jewel—a veritable jewel. I found it in a telegram from Linz, and it contains ninety-five letters:*
>
> *Personaleinkommensteuerschatzungskommissionsmitglied-sreisekostenrechnungserganzungsrevisionsfund*
>
> *If I could get a similar word engraved upon my tombstone I should sleep beneath it in peace.*

Write Now

Oscar Wilde once wrote: "I never travel without my diary. One should always have something sensational to read on the train."

Write a diary, journal, or blog entry on one of the following subjects (your diary entry doesn't have to be sensational!):

❧ What is one of your qualities that you especially like?

❧ If you could have any superpower, which one would it be and why?

❧ How would you change the world to make it a better place?

❧ What did you do yesterday?

❧ If you could be any historical figure, who would you be and why?

❧ What is something that you do well? Describe your skill.

❧ If you had to describe yourself as an animal, which animal would you be and why?

❧ Describe your favorite holiday or celebration.

❧ If you could go anywhere in the world, where would you go and why? Who would you bring with you? Why?

❧ How would your life change if you won a $50 million lottery tomorrow?

You Must Remember This

You can write for many reasons. These include self-discovery, reaching out to others, and expressing your feelings. Perhaps you will write creatively to heal past wounds, to leave a legacy for future generations, or to evaluate something. No matter what your reasons for being a creative writer, your writing will make the world a better place.

$\mathscr{C}$HAPTER 3
Sources of Inspiration

—⧴⧵—

I often speak at writing conferences, national conventions, and book signings, where I get asked a lot of questions, of course, the most frequent one being: "Where do you get your ideas?" Where *do* creative writers get their inspiration? That's what you'll discover in this chapter.

I'll share some ways to get inspiration that work for many creative writers, including me. Pick and choose the ones that appeal to you. If you find yourself getting writer's block, try a different method of sparking ideas. Very often that will unlock your creativity.

You Can Always Call on the Greek Muses
To the Greeks, inspiration came directly from the gods. (They weren't kidding—the word *inspiration* literally means "god-breathed.") The Greeks believed that specific gods, called Muses, could be called on for specific artistic inspiration. It was a simple plan: you'd just call on the Muse you needed. For instance, you want to write epic poetry? Calliope is your Muse. Are you blocked while writing a tragedy? Give Melpomene a call. Euterpe could inspire would-be writers of lyric song; Thalia was the go-to gal for comedy and poetry about nature. There was even a Muse for erotic poetry, Erato. Those Greeks knew how to get inspiration for creative writing.

Write Now
The Greek Muses are a bit shopworn. Besides, everyone needs a personal muse, so why not invent your own? List the muse's qual-

ities and the type of creative writing the muse inspires. Explain why this particular muse is ideal for you.

Get Emotional
To the followers of Freudian psychology, inspiration comes from the artist's inner psyche. The actual inspiration springs from unresolved childhood trauma or psychological strife. Thus, Freudians consider the artist wounded and unquestionably unique.

Nature Inspires Creativity
Now, I'm not asking you to walk across burning coals or be impaled on a bed of nails for art's sake, but it *is* undeniable that a great deal of creative writing springs from strong emotions. When we're in love, when we're ill or injured, when we're thrilled by a wonderful experience, or when we're despairing at a setback we often feel inspired to capture our emotions in words. Poet William Wordsworth was inspired when he saw a gorgeous field of daffodils. Here's his famous poem "I Wandered Lonely as a Cloud." As you read it, think about what emotions a field of flowers would spark in you.

> I wandered lonely as a cloud
> That floats on high o'er vales and hills,
> When all at once I saw a crowd,
> A host, of golden daffodils;
> Beside the lake, beneath the trees,
> Fluttering and dancing in the breeze.
>
> Continuous as the stars that shine
> And twinkle on the milky way,
> They stretched in never-ending line
> Along the margin of a bay:
> Ten thousand saw I at a glance,
> Tossing their heads in sprightly dance.
>
> The waves beside them danced; but they
> Out-did the sparkling waves in glee:
> A poet could not but be gay,
> In such a jocund company:
> I gazed—and gazed—but little thought
> What wealth the show to me had brought:

For oft, when on my couch I lie
In vacant or in pensive mood,
They flash upon that inward eye
Which is the bliss of solitude;
And then my heart with pleasure fills,
And dances with the daffodils.

Love Inspires Creativity

Shakespeare wrote the following lyric poem, Sonnet 18, in the grip of strong emotion: love. In this sonnet, he first compares his beloved to the traditional beauties of nature. He concludes with an especially comforting idea: his beloved will live forever. How is this possible? Credit the power of creative writing: the poem will ensure his beloved's immortality. And so it has.

Shall I compare thee to a summer's day?
Thou art more lovely and more temperate:
Rough winds do shake the darling buds of May,
And summer's lease hath all too short a date:
Sometime too hot the eye of heaven shines,
And often is his gold complexion dimm'd;
And every fair from fair sometime declines,
By chance or nature's changing course untrimm'd;
But thy eternal summer shall not fade
Nor lose possession of that fair thou owest;
Nor shall Death brag thou wander'st in his shade,
When in eternal lines to time thou growest:
So long as men can breathe or eyes can see,
So long lives this and this gives life to thee.

A *sonnet* is a fourteen-line lyric poem, written in iambic pentameter. There are two traditional forms: the Italian and the English sonnet. In the *Italian (Petrarchan) sonnet*, the first eight lines, called the octave, rhyme abba/abba and present the subject/conflict; the final six lines, called the sestet, rhyme cde/cde and resolve the problem. In the *English (Shakespearean) sonnet*, the lines rhyme abab/cdcd/efef/gg. The final two lines, a couplet, sum up the main idea and often present a memorable insight.

Look into Your Soul

If you're having trouble picking a topic to spark your artistic vision, think about the following questions. Each one evokes a strong emotion:

- ❧ Who or what do you love?

- ❧ Who or what do you hate?

- ❧ Who or what makes you very angry?

- ❧ Who or what fills you with joy?

- ❧ What are your wildest dreams?

- ❧ What are your biggest fears?

Write Now

Write a brief poem about being in love. Your poem can describe the agony or the ecstasy of love, its depths or its heights. Your poem can be funny or tragic, light or heavy. Whatever form, tone, or approach you choose, write from your soul.

Get Out More!

"Don't be a busybody!" you were told as a child. "Stop listening at doors! Mind your own business." Well, when it comes to inspiration for creative writing, take your inspiration from here, there, and everywhere. For instance, one day while riding on a bus, mystery writer Agatha Christie overheard someone say to a friend, "Why didn't they ask Evans?" This tiny snippet of conversation was enough to spark Christie's imagination, resulting in a novel of the same name.

Her book *The Secret Adversary* stemmed from a conversation she overheard in a tea shop. Christie put it this way: "Two people were talking at a table nearby, discussing somebody called Jane Fish. . . . That, I thought, would make a good beginning to a story—a name overheard at a tea shop—an unusual name, so that whoever heard it remembered it." *Murder on the Links* was prompted by a newspaper article that Christie read about a suspicious murder in France.

> Of course, I am not telling you to listen in at keyholes, steam open mail, or hide under the bed to get the salacious gossip. But then again, creative writers *do* have to be creative in getting their ideas!

Travel on the Cheap

Christie didn't confine herself to overhearing other people's conversations while riding on the bus or sitting in tea shops, however. She was also an active and intrepid traveler. She especially enjoyed accompanying her husband, Max Mallowan, on his archaeological digs to Asia and the Middle East. These trips gave her the inspiration for her classic detective story *Murder on the Orient Express* as well several other mystery novels that she set in exotic locales.

"I can't afford a weekend at the shore, much less travel on the Orient Express," you say. You don't have give up the inspiration that a change of scenery brings if your job, budget, or family constraints make travel difficult or impossible. As a creative writer, you can get inspiration from virtual travel as well as actual journeys. Try these ideas:

❧ Watch television shows and movies set in foreign lands. Pay close attention to the landscape, customs, and culture you see.

❧ Read books, stories, poems, and other literature that takes place in unfamiliar settings. Think about how you might adapt these details to your own writing.

❧ Read nonfiction about faraway places. Archaeological and nature magazines are great for inspiration.

❧ Look at fine art, especially paintings and drawings created in different cultures and time periods.

❧ Interview people who have traveled. Listen to their recollections.

❧ Attend travelers' lectures. Travelers often speak for free
in libraries, civic groups, and schools. The speakers show
slides, posters, and other visuals to illustrate their adventures.

File It Away

To make sure that you remember your fascinating experiences as
an actual or virtual traveler, keep an idea book. Get a large journal. In it, jot down ideas and potential plots and characters as they
come to you. Here are some other things to keep in your idea
book as well:

e-mail	photographs
greeting cards	postcards
letters	snippets of conversation
newspaper clippings	your own sketches and drawings

Look to Other Writers

As a result of the emotion that infuses it, creative writing opens a
window into your soul. Your reader learns more about you as a
result of your words. Creative writing can also hold up a mirror—
in a metaphorical sense—so that your reader might learn something about themselves. How often have you read an essay, blog
entry, short story, or other creative work of literature and said,
"The writer knows just how I feel! It's as if the author is writing
about me." If the writing sparks that sense of identification in you,
it will likely get your imagination flowing as well.

As a result, one of the best sources of inspiration comes from
other writers. William Shakespeare is a case in point. To create one
of his funniest comedies, *The Taming of the Shrew*, Shakespeare
drew on many sources. The shrewish woman (opinionated, dom-
ineering, and forthright in her opinions) comes from folklore. For
instance, Noah's wife was portrayed this way in the medieval mystery plays. Other sources Shakespeare used included George
Gascoigne's play *Supposes* (1566), which Gascoigne himself based
on Ludovico Ariosto's *I Suppositi* (1509). *That* play comes from
the classical Latin comedies of Plautus and Terence. And that's
not all! The opening of *The Taming of the Shrew* comes from *The
Arabian Nights*.

Much, much later—1949, to be exact—Samuel and Bella

Spewack and Cole Porter looked to *The Taming of the Shrew* as inspiration for their musical *Kiss Me, Kate*. Their award-winning humorous play tells the story of two musical comedy actors, once married to each other but now divorced, who are performing opposite each other in the roles of Petruchio and Katharine in a musical version of *The Taming of the Shrew*.

It's no secret that writers are influenced by the works of those who came before them. Nobel Prize winning–novelist Ernest Hemingway paid homage to the influence of Mark Twain when he said, "All modern American literature comes from one book by Mark Twain called Huckleberry Finn."

What inspiration can you get from other writers? How can drawing on the work of other writers help you become a better writer? Read widely; read voraciously. What should you do if you don't know where to start? Below is my list of novels that inspire writers because of their themes, writing styles, characters, settings, and plots. Why not read or reread some of them?

Eighty-five Best Novels of All Times (according to Dr. Rozakis)

1. *1984* by George Orwell
2. *The Adventures of Augie March* by Saul Bellow
3. *The Adventures of Huckleberry Finn* by Mark Twain
4. *The Age of Innocence* by Edith Wharton
5. *All Quiet on the Western Front* by Erich Maria Remarque
6. *All the King's Men* by Robert Penn Warren
7. *The American* by Henry James
8. *An American Tragedy* by Theodore Dreiser
9. *Animal Farm* by George Orwell
10. *As I Lay Dying* by William Faulkner
11. *The Awakening* by Kate Chopin
12. *Beloved* by Toni Morrison
13. *Brave New World* by Aldous Huxley
14. *The Call of the Wild* by Jack London
15. *Catch-22* by Joseph Heller
16. *A Christmas Carol* by Charles Dickens
17. *A Confederacy of Dunces* by John Kennedy Toole
18. *The Count of Monte Cristo* by Alexandre Dumas
19. *Crime and Punishment* by Fyodor Dostoevsky
20. *David Copperfield* by Charles Dickens

21. *The Day of the Locust* by Nathanael West
22. *Death Comes for the Archbishop* by Willa Cather
23. *Don Quixote* by Miguel de Cervantes
24. *Dracula* by Bram Stoker
25. *Ethan Frome* by Edith Wharton
26. *Fahrenheit 451* by Ray Bradbury
27. *Flowers for Algernon* by Daniel Keyes
28. *The Foundation Trilogy* by Isaac Asimov
29. *Frankenstein* by Mary Shelley
30. *From Here to Eternity* by James Jones
31. *Gone With the Wind* by Margaret Mitchell
32. *The Grapes of Wrath* by John Steinbeck
33. *Gravity's Rainbow* by Thomas Pynchon
34. *Great Expectations* by Charles Dickens
35. *The Great Gatsby* by F. Scott Fitzgerald
36. *Gulliver's Travels* by Jonathan Swift
37. *Henderson the Rain King* by Saul Bellow
38. *The Hound of the Baskervilles* by Sir Arthur Conan Doyle
39. *A House for Mr. Biswas* by V. S. Naipaul
40. *Howards End* by E. M. Forster
41. *The Hunchback of Notre Dame* by Victor Hugo
42. *In Cold Blood* by Truman Capote
43. *Invisible Man* by Ralph Ellison
44. *Jane Eyre* by Charlotte Brontë
45. *The Jungle* by Upton Sinclair
46. *Little Women* by Louisa May Alcott
47. *Lolita* by Vladimir Nabokov
48. *The Magic Mountain* by Thomas Mann
49. *Main Street* by Sinclair Lewis
50. *The Mayor of Casterbridge* by Thomas Hardy
51. *Les Misérables* by Victor Hugo
52. *Moby Dick* by Herman Melville
53. *The Moviegoer* by Walker Percy
54. *The Murder of Roger Ackroyd* by Agatha Christie
55. *My Ántonia* by Willa Cather
56. *The Naked and the Dead* by Norman Mailer
57. *Native Son* by Richard Wright
58. *Parade's End* by Ford Madox Ford
59. *A Passage to India* by E. M. Forster

60. *The Plague* by Albert Camus
61. *Portnoy's Complaint* by Philip Roth
62. *A Portrait of the Artist as a Young Man* by James Joyce
63. *The Postman Always Rings Twice* by James M. Cain
64. *Pride and Prejudice* by Jane Austen
65. *The Red Badge of Courage* by Stephen Crane
66. *Remembrance of Things Past* by Marcel Proust
67. *The Scarlet Letter* by Nathaniel Hawthorne
68. *The Secret Garden* by Frances Hodgson Burnett
69. *Silas Marner* by George Eliot
70. *Sister Carrie* by Theodore Dreiser
71. *Sons and Lovers* by D. H. Lawrence
72. *Sophie's Choice* by William Styron
73. *The Sound and the Fury* by William Faulkner
74. *The Sun Also Rises* by Ernest Hemingway
75. *The Tale of Genji* by Shikibu Murasaki
76. *To Kill a Mockingbird* by Harper Lee
77. *To the Lighthouse* by Virginia Woolf
78. *Treasure Island* by Robert Louis Stevenson
79. *The Trial* by Franz Kafka
80. *Uncle Tom's Cabin* by Harriet Beecher Stowe
81. *Winesburg, Ohio* by Sherwood Anderson
82. *Wise Blood* by Flannery O'Connor
83. *The Wonderful Wizard of Oz* by L. Frank Baum
84. *Wuthering Heights* by Emily Brontë
85. *Zen and the Art of Motorcycle Maintenance* by Robert M. Pirsig

Write Now
Write a brief journal, diary, or blog entry about a book that has had a major influence on your writing. Explain how the book inspired you to become a creative writer.

Take the Plunge!
Perhaps you think that you don't have enough talent to be a creative writer. "All the inspiration and reading in the world aren't going to make a difference," you think. "I just don't have the ability to be a creative writer." Pish-tosh. Talk yourself into failing, and you most likely will. Talk yourself into succeeding, and you will.

It's true that some people have a greater facility with language than others. Nonetheless, just as anyone can learn to cook a gourmet meal or add a column of numbers, so anyone can learn to write well. Make this your maxim: *With inspiration and determination, I can be a creative writer.*

The Canterbury Tales ranks as one of the greatest epic works of world literature. Chaucer made a crucial contribution to English literature in using English at a time when much court poetry was still written in Anglo-Norman or Latin. When you have the time, check out the *Tales*: the stories therein provide not only perceptive insights into the human psyche, but they are also bawdy and funny. The combination results in a great source of inspiration.

Outside responsibilities and age aren't factors, either. You are never too busy to become a creative writer. And you are never too young or too old to become a creative writer. For instance, full-time diplomat and courtier Geoffrey Chaucer (c. 1343–1400) started his *Canterbury Tales* when he was fifty-four years old; he finished when he was sixty-one. Full-time farmer Laura Ingalls Wilder didn't start writing her *Little House* series of children's books until she was in her sixties. The nine novels were her first books, too.

You don't need many supplies to be a creative writer—just some paper and a writing tool. And you don't need a fancy education, either. A surprisingly large number of successful creative writers never completed their formal education. British novelist Charles Dickens, American humorist Mark Twain, Russian novelist Maxim Gorky, Irish writer Seán O'Casey, and Italian novelist Alberto Moravia never finished grammar school. Of course you shouldn't shun education if you want to be a creative writer. But you can succeed as a writer without having a shiny two-hundred-thousand-dollar college diploma on your wall.

> The first English woman to earn her living as an author seems to have been Aphra Behn (1640–89). She wrote several plays, poems, and novels, including such tales of adventure and romance as *The Fair Jilt, The Rover,* and *Sylvia.*

Some Easy Suggestions

Are you frustrated by the number of factors that conspire to keep you from writing? If so, you're not alone. You start out thinking it's just a simple matter of sitting down and writing the essay, story, or blog that you have wanted to write for a long time. Then you think, "How do I get started?" "What form does this have to be in?" "Should I type or handwrite my work?" By the time you finish second-guessing yourself, you're too upset even to consider writing.

Below are some suggestions to get you started writing. After you finish reading these ideas, why not take half an hour and put your thoughts down on paper.

Aim for the Stars

Don't sell yourself short; dare to dream. Creative writing, like anything else worth doing, is a risk. But you're up to the challenge. Tell yourself that you will be a failure and you very likely will be. Tell yourself that you'll be a success and you'll soar.

I believe in you; now believe in yourself.

Decide to Make Writing a Priority

You find time for everyone else; why not find some time for yourself? You can make a little more time by learning the art of saying no every now and again. I did it and so can you. Here's how I accomplished this seemingly impossible feat: I ran my daughter's Girl Scout troop for seven years. While I enjoyed it very much, it did really eat into my time. Finally I got the courage to say, "No more. I put in my time—all seven years of it. Get a new leader." People were initially astonished. "How can you leave the girls in the lurch?" they wailed. "I need some time for myself," I answered. In the wink of an eye, another mother stepped in to fill my shoes. At first I felt a twinge of resentment; after all, how could I be so quickly replaced? Then I felt a great sense of relief—and I had several more hours a week to devote to writing.

"I can't set aside the time to write just now," you say. "I'll do it in the future." I have to (pick one):

make breakfast	take the iguana for a walk
get to my job	learn to keyboard
do the food shopping	clean the house
finish my college degree	call the super for the bath-
get the oil in my car	room leak
changed	help my aged parents

You do have many very important demands on your time. Unfortunately, you will always have demands on your time; the specific demands might change, but you'll always be pulled in different directions.

The future is now. As the writer Barbara Kingsolver said, "There is no perfect time to write. There's only now."

Practice Pays Big Dividends

Writing is like anything else: the more you put in, the more you get out. The more you write, the better you get. The better you get, the more pleasure writing will bring. So get started!

Follow Your Bliss

Write what gives you pleasure. For example, perhaps you've always wanted to write your memoir. So do it! Maybe you want to express your individuality in essays or perhaps in short stories. Select the form and content that satisfy and soothe your soul.

Then close the door. Write all alone, with no one looking over your shoulder, tugging at your leg, or calling for a ride to the mall. When the novelist Barbara Rogan is writing, she instructs her children not to disturb her unless the house is on fire. And so she has produced an impressive number of wonderful books—as well as two wonderful sons who respect and admire her work.

Don't try to figure out what other people want to hear from you; figure out what you have to say. It's the something unique you have to offer.

Learn from the Best

You've no doubt noticed that I've sprinkled examples of fine writing throughout this chapter as well as the entire book. I've also done quite a bit of name-dropping, listing creative writers from all over the world and down through the ages. I've included poets and essayists, short story writers and novelists.

It was done quite deliberately, because one of the best ways to become a fine writer is to be a fine reader. The more writing models you study, the easier it will be for you to find your own unique voice.

As Allan W. Eckert said, "If you would be a writer, first be a reader. Only through the assimilation of ideas, thoughts and philosophies can one begin to focus his own ideas, thoughts and philosophies."

Enjoy Yourself

Writing has brought *me* enormous joy, as it has for untold writers around the world and through the ages. Wright Morris notes that "Writing has made me rich—not in money but in a couple hundred characters out there, whose pursuits and anguish and triumphs I've shared. I am unspeakably grateful at the life I have come to lead." Get a little of that pleasure—or a lot—by letting your creativity and talent soar.

You Must Remember This

Dear Reader, as you embark on your journey of creative writing, remember Emily Dickinson's originality and determination.

> "Hope" is the thing with feathers—
> That perches in the soul—
> And sings the tune without the words—
> And never stops—at all—

CHAPTER 4
The Process of Writing

—⟨∞∞⟩—

Has a writer friend ever said to you, "Oh, writing is a snap. The words come so easily. I don't put any work into it at all." Hm . . . I'd take another look at *that* friendship if I were you. Do you get upset because everyone you know seems to write effortlessly? (Not to mention professional writers—bet the words just flow for them.)

Here's the truth: the words don't flow magically for anyone. The people who claim that they do are also the ones who say, "Oh, I never diet!" and "Yes, my hair has always been this color."

We know that successful writers follow a specific process when they write. Learning the steps in this process can help you write more easily and effectively, although all good writing requires effort. That's what you'll learn in this chapter.

Let's Take the Mystery Out of Creative Writing
Some people like to make things more difficult than they have to be, and some people like to make things easier. I'm in the latter camp. You don't have to open a vein to be a creative writer. As with any process, writing can be divided into a series of steps. It doesn't matter whether you're writing an essay or a blog entry, a short story or a letter, the same steps hold true. Different writers have slightly different steps, so I'll teach you the six steps that have worked well for me. Knowing this process gives you a way to approach any type of creative writing. This makes it easier to get started—and to finish your projects.

There are many advantages to knowing this process. Here are three of the most important ones:

1. You can focus on one part of the writing process at a time, which will help you stay on track.
2. You'll keep writing and get your ideas down on paper.
3. You'll avoid writer's block and panic over "Where do I go next?"

Always think of the writing process as a series of suggestions, not a clear-cut road map. As you get more comfortable with the steps, you'll be able to vary them, as you do when you prepare a familiar recipe. Perhaps you'll add a little more time here and take away a little there. You might want to combine two steps or double back and complete the same step twice. You may skip some steps, too. Remember: use the writing process to help you write more easily and freely. Adapt it to suit your own needs and desires. That said, here's the process in brief:

How to Tackle Any Type of Creative Writing
Here are the six steps in the writing process:

1. Planning your writing
2. Narrowing your subject
3. Researching your topic
4. Writing your drafts
5. Polishing your manuscript
6. Proofreading the finished writing

Here's what each step involves:

1. *Planning your writing*
   - ❧ Figuring out why you are writing
   - ❧ Deciding who will read your writing
   - ❧ Choosing something to write about

2. *Narrowing your subject*
   - ❧ Selecting the specific angle or focus
   - ❧ Making a graphic organizer, such as a web, chart, outline, or storyboard
   - ❧ Choosing a method of organization

3. *Researching your topic*
   - ❧ Thinking about what you already know
   - ❧ Finding the additional information you need
   - ❧ Jotting down facts, details, and examples

4. *Writing your drafts*
   - ❧ Deciding on the form your writing will take
   - ❧ Determining what to include and what to leave out
   - ❧ Writing the first few versions

5. *Polishing your manuscript*
   - ❧ Adding, deleting, and rearranging words, sentences, and paragraphs
   - ❧ Correcting errors in skills (usage, grammar, mechanics, spelling, capitalization)
   - ❧ Rewriting confusing or erroneous sentences
   - ❧ Getting comments and suggestions from editors
   - ❧ Checking length and format

6. *Proofreading the finished writing*
   - ❧ Correcting typographical errors
   - ❧ Adding any missing punctuation
   - ❧ Checking that every word is there

Now, let's look at each step in detail. This will help you understand how you can make the writing process work for you.

Planning Your Writing
The wonderful part of writing is that you don't have to get it right the first time, unlike, say, brain surgery. You can always refine your

writing by inserting a more precise word, a more apt phrase, a more vivid figure of speech. If you think of the writing process this way, it will help relieve any pressure you might feel. Once you know you can *always* rethink the direction, details, and descriptions, you can write with greater ease and confidence. Start by planning what you want to accomplish in a specific writing.

Your plan can be long or short, simple or complex. It can be anything *you* want, as long as it helps you figure out where you're going with a particular writing. For example, Charles Dickens always took the time to plan his novels, even though he then wrote very quickly. Below is a small part of Dickens's plan for a chapter in his novel *Little Dorrit:*

A Plea in The Marshalsea

Ever downward, always downward

Clennam Ill

Little Dorrit's return, and her offer

Arthur's refusal of Little

Scene between her and Arthur *

D's offer

*Close with John Chivery stealing in
at night, to bring her "undying love" to him.*

It's brief, even sketchy, but this plan helped Dickens make some important decisions about his plot and characters. This plan also illustrates a very important point about planning: only *you* have to understand the plan. That's because *it's for your eyes only.* (When your writing becomes famous, your plans might get published, but that's another story.)

As you plan a specific piece of writing, think about why you are writing, who will read your writing, and what you will write about. Let's look at these three elements more closely.

Figuring Out Why You Are Writing

As you learned in chapter 2, you have seven main reasons for writing: for self-discovery, to reach out to others, to express your feelings, for healing, for future generations, to evaluate something, and to entertain others. Your writing may have one purpose or several. The decision is yours.

Deciding Who Will Read Your Writing

You might be writing for children or adults, friends or strangers. You might be writing for your neighbor, your boss, or your child's teacher. Your reader might even be yourself, especially if you are writing a journal for healing or self-discovery. Your reader determines the words you use and how you arrange them. For example, if your readers are children, you would use shorter, easier words than if you were writing for adults. If you are writing for people on the job, you might use a lot of technical words and expressions that only workers in that particular occupation would understand.

Choosing Something to Write About

One of the glories of creative writing is the subject: you get to pick whatever subject you want. When you are writing on the job, in contrast, you are often given a subject that you must explore. Take the time to find something worth writing about, something that you feel passionate about. Then decide on the specific angle or focus you want. Aim for a slant that interests you as well as your readers. If you are very enthusiastic about a subject, your writing will reflect this and carry readers along with your joy.

Narrowing Your Subject

Early in his career, Charles Dickens wrote to a friend about the excitement of narrowing a subject. He said: "I can never write with effect—especially in the serious way—until I have got my steam up, or in other words until I have become so excited with my subject that I cannot leave off!" As Charles Dickens realized, when your subject takes hold of you, it can be almost impossible to *stop* writing.

But some subjects are just too big to tackle. For example, you might not have the time to write an entire history of World War II or be able to squeeze it all into a short story. In that case, you have to narrow the topic so it fits your space and time limitations.

Suppose you want to write a poem about your personality and character. You've learned about the main elements you must consider. Here they are, applied to this particular writing task:

❧ Why I am writing   for self-discovery

❧ Who will read my writing   adults

❧ What I am writing about   myself

How can you narrow your subject? Given these limits, you decide to describe three of your character traits. To show what you're planning, you can make any kind of visual, such as a chart, web, outline, or storyboard. As you saw in the previous example, Charles Dickens made a brief outline. You decide to make a chart. Here's what it looks like:

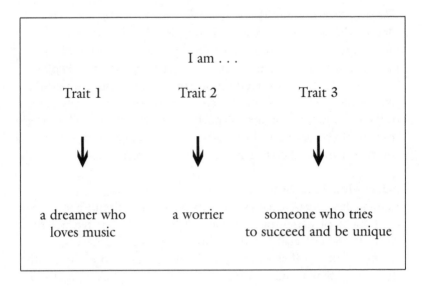

Here's what the same information looks like in a web:

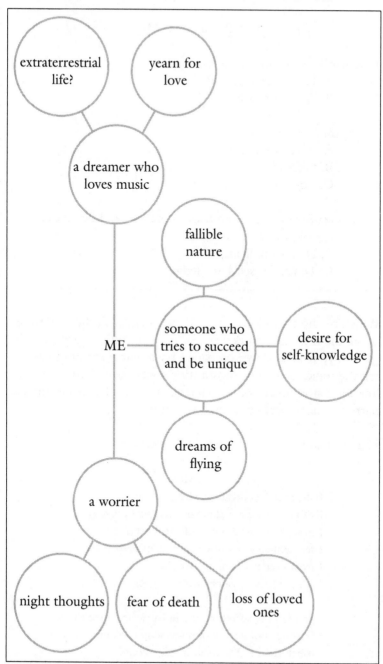

As an outline:

A Poem about Me

I. Stanza 1: A dreamer who loves music
    A. Extraterrestrial life?
    B. Yearn for love

II. Stanza 2: A worrier
    A. Night thoughts
    B. Fears of death
    C. Loss of loved ones

III. Stanza 3: Someone who tries to succeed and be unique
    A. Fallible nature
    B. Dreams of flying
    C. Desire for self-knowledge

Which method should you use? Experiment with them all to discover the ones that work best for you. If you're having trouble getting your ideas down on paper, try a new method of narrowing the topic. Often just substituting a web for a chart, or an outline for a storyboard, or any change at all will free your mind to narrow your subject in exciting new ways.

Here's what the finished poem looks like:

Me

I am a restless dreamer who loves music.
I wonder if we are alone in this great universe.
I hear the choked music of the world.
I see faint smiles in the darkness of despair.
I want everlasting, true love.
I am a restless dreamer who loves music.

I pretend the secrets of the universe are open to me.
I feel the cool fingers of night wisp across my room.
I touch the brightest star in the infinite sky.

I worry my life is finite.
I cry for those who found theirs was.
I am a restless dreamer who loves music.

I understand I am not perfect.
I say, "I can try."
I dream of flying to the vast heavens.
I try to be myself.
I hope to learn just what "myself" is.
I am a restless dreamer who loves music.

Researching Your Topic

Where do you get the descriptions that give life to your subject? When you're writing *fiction* (short stories and novels, for example), you create the information from your imagination. Drawing from what you've seen and heard, you weave a tale of wonder. When you're writing *nonfiction* (such as biographies, essays, and memoirs), you might use facts that other people have gathered.

What happens if you don't have details you need? Perhaps you're not sure what a certain place is like. You might never have experienced the smell of the heather on an English moor, for instance. If you are writing about a real place, you can travel there to experience it firsthand or watch a video of it. If you are writing about an imaginary place, you might visit some real places to gather different impressions to use. When you do so, you're conducting one type of *research*.

> *Fiction* is imaginative narration; *nonfiction* is factual writing. Novels and short stories are fiction; essays, articles, biographies, and autobiographies are nonfiction. Please don't ever say that you've written a "fictional novel" or a "fictional tale" because you're saying the same thing twice!

In 1895, the American writer Stephen Crane published *The Red Badge of Courage*, a brutally realistic account of the impact of war on a young recruit, Henry Fleming. A vivid tale of what Crane called "the red sickness of battle," *The Red Badge of Courage* is now ranked as *the* classic novel of the Civil War. Crane was twen-

ty-four years old when he published *The Red Badge of Courage.*
The Civil War had ended a decade before his birth. He had never
fought in a war or even seen a battle. How could someone with
no firsthand experience of war create such a convincing war novel?
Part of the answer lies with the quality of Crane's research. Today
much of this material is easily available on the Internet, which
makes the task of gathering it easier, faster, and more fun.

> Just because a "source" appears in print, in the media,
> or online doesn't mean it is valid. As a result, you must
> evaluate every source critically and carefully before you
> use it.

No matter which sources you use, take careful notes. You can
do this any way that works for you, longhand or on a computer.
Many writers also include pictures, postcards, sketches, and other
visuals to help them remember key details. Carefully document all
sources so you can properly credit them in the text or in the back
of the book.

Writing Your Drafts

In 1852, Charles Dickens wrote a letter to his fellow novelist
Wilkie Collins. In the letter, Dickens described "the conceited
idiots who suppose that volumes are tossed off like pancakes, and
that any writing can be done without the utmost application, the
greatest patience, and the steadiest energy of which the writer is
capable."

Charles Dickens knew that writing isn't like making a tossed
salad. Rather, all the ideas have to be carefully arranged in an
organized, logical way. The way you select is completely up to
you. It's determined by your readers, your subject, your purpose,
and your writing style. Will you present your ideas in a blog or an
essay? Will you open your narrative with dialogue, a quotation, or
action? It's all your choice, one of the joys of being a writer.

> When you *draft* your writing, you are creating rough
> copies.

Drafting

Now, how do you actually sit down and start to turn all your ideas into a unified whole? There's no one right way to write. The important thing is to find the method that works with your personality and writing task. Here are some methods you may wish to try:

- ✒ *Drafting Method 1:* Use your charts, webs, other visuals, and notes as a framework for your first draft. Adhere very closely to these notes. Start at the beginning and work through everything. Try to write at a steady pace until you reach a natural breaking point, such as the end of a chapter, stanza, or incident.

- ✒ *Drafting Method 2:* Read through all your planning material and then set it aside. Try to write your draft in one sitting to maintain a single impression or effect, but feel free to jump around the piece as different ideas occur. Obviously, this method works best with small projects (such as poems) or chunks of larger projects (such as chapters in a novel).

- ✒ *Drafting Method 3:* Write without notes and visuals. Instead, just start freewriting by letting your ideas flow without brakes. Then look for links among ideas and explore these ideas.

Remember, you're not under any obligation to use all or even part of your first draft. This realization can free you to explore new directions as you write.

Stick to It!

How many rough drafts will you have to write to get your words the way you want? The answer depends on your writing style, the subject you have chosen, and how much time you have to rework your ideas. Some people write with lightning speed; others, with glacial slowness.

Shakespeare, not surprisingly, was known as a very fast writer. "His mind and hand went together," his publishers Heminges and Condell reported, "and what he thought, he uttered with that easiness that we have scarce received from him a blot in his papers." But other writers are not that fortunate.

Virgil took ten years to write the *Aeneid* and believed it still needed about three years' work when he died. Katherine Anne Porter worked on *Ship of Fools* for over twenty years; it took Harold Brodkey thirty-one years to finish his novel *Runaway Soul*. The classic American poet Walt Whitman wrote only one book, the landmark collection *Leaves of Grass*. He issued the first edition in 1855 and worked on the book steadily through eight editions. The last version was issued in 1892, appropriately called the death bed edition.

> On average, writers spend about one third of their time shaping and drafting their writing, but there is no fixed rule on how to allocate your time.

Polishing Your Manuscript

Even though Charles Dickens wrote an impressive stream of novels, letters, and articles, he was always a very careful writer. He paid very close attention to the smallest aspects of style and structure. Even the smallest detail wasn't beneath his notice.

For example, Dickens wanted to make his characters individual and memorable. To do so, he gave each character a fitting (and often funny) name. Here are his notes concerning the name for the title character in his novel *Martin Chuzzlewit:*

> *chevy* ~~Slyme Slyme Esquire~~
> ~~Mr. Flick~~
> ~~Mr. Sweetlefee.~~
> *Young Martin Chuzzlewit*

As with all skilled writers, Charles Dickens recognized the importance of going back over a draft and reworking it. Here's what professional writer Roger Verhulst said about the importance of revising and editing:

I wish I could write briskly and beautifully and never have to touch a word more than once, but that almost never happens to me. I am never entirely sure, while I'm working on it, just what feel or tone a finished article is going to have. So I can't tell along the way whether the words I'm using at the moment are going to fit.

Once a piece is roughed out, the process becomes a bit easier, but even then I do a lot of reworking. I console myself for having been denied the gift of inspiration by telling myself that this time-consuming process of reworking and refining distinguishes the professional writer from the nonprofessional.

If everything that first tumbled from the ends of my fingertips were the best I could do, I would starve as a writer. I like to think that I have learned enough about writing to recognize a problem when I see it, and to know a little how to fix it.

As Roger Verhulst explains, your first draft won't be perfect, and probably the second, third, and fourth drafts won't be, either. But that's fine, because you can always revise and edit your work. In fact, you surely will because all good writers do. Don't be shocked if your revised draft bears little resemblance to your first draft.

Blood, Sweat, and Tears
What do writers do when they revise and edit? Depending on your individual writing style and the amount of time you have set aside for this step in the writing process, you will do some or all of the following things:

❧ Add words, sentences, and paragraphs necessary to clarify meaning

❧ Delete words, sentences, and paragraphs that don't fit at all

❧ Rearrange words, sentences, and paragraphs for logic and unity

❧ Rewrite awkward sentences for clarity

❧ Rework inaccurate or misleading statements

❧ Cut or expand the writing to fit the space requirements

❧ Adjust the tone to fit the subject and readers

❧ Change the point of view (say from the first person *I* to the third person *they*)

❧ Gather comments and suggestions from editors. Your editors can be family members, friends, fellow writers, or professional editors, for example

❧ Correct errors in spelling, usage, grammar, and mechanics

> The *tone* of a work of literature is the writer's attitude toward his or her subject matter. For example, the tone can be angry, bitter, sad, or frightening.

Steps in the Polishing Process
Follow these steps as you polish your writing:

❧ Let your draft sit for a few hours, a few days, or even longer. Getting some distance from your writing will help you see where you want to make changes.

❧ Then read your draft once all the way through.

❧ Evaluate your writing to decide which parts are strong and which ones need to be reworked. You may even decide to redraft instead of revising this draft.

❧ If you decide to revise, focus on one issue at a time. For example, first read for plot, next for unity, then for characterization, and so on.

❧ Make a checklist geared to your particular needs. Base the items on your readers, purpose, and subject as well as on your own strengths and weaknesses. For instance, if you have problems with openings, focus on the beginning of each paragraph.

❧ Consider what your readers have said. As you weigh their comments, try to separate yourself from your work to judge the validity of their assessments. Try not to be defensive. If the feedback is negative, don't take it personally.

❧ Read your writing aloud. Hearing your words can help you find things you might have missed. You can also use a tape recorder for this purpose. Read your writing into the tape recorder. Then play the tape over and over, listening for different elements each time.

❧ Learn from your success. Compare this particular effort with similar ones to see what you've done well. This can help you build on your strengths.

Above all, don't get discouraged. Rome wasn't built in a day. Even Shakespeare took some time to get it right. As writer Roberta Gellis says: "Dreaming and hoping won't produce a piece of work; only writing, rewriting and rewriting (if necessary)—a devoted translation of thoughts and dreams into words on paper—will result in a story."

Proofreading the Finished Writing

You wouldn't leave the house without glancing in the mirror and patting that stray strand of hair in place. In the same way, you'd never turn in a piece of writing that hadn't been carefully proofread. Even if you're pressed for time, *always proofread your writing before you submit it for any kind of publication*—online, on the job, or in the print media.

When you proofread your writing, look for errors in spelling, punctuation, grammar, and usage. We're creatures of habit, so we're most likely to make the same writing mistakes over and over. For instance, you might have problems remembering how to spell common homonyms such as *their, there, they're* or *dessert, desert.* To make the most of your time, check for these errors first—but don't neglect all the other typos that often slip by.

As you proofread, try these suggestions:

❧ Start by running a spell-checker. Recognize, however, that a spell-checker won't pick up words that are misused, such as *ion* or *inn* for *in*. (I make that typo a lot.)

❧ Then read the document for meaning. Make sure that you haven't omitted any words, for example.

❧ Look for typographical errors.

❧ Double-check numbers, names, and dates.

❧ Pay special attention to words in large type. The bigger a word, the more likely it is to look correct when it's wrong.

❧ Ask a friend to proofread your writing after you've checked it over once or twice.

You Must Remember This

Writing is a process that can be mastered with instruction, practice, and concentration. The steps in the writing process include planning your writing, narrowing and researching your topic, shaping and drafting your words, revising and editing your manuscript, and proofreading the finished product. You may follow all these steps in this order, or select the ones you need. You can also vary the order of steps, even doubling back and repeating several steps, as necessary.

CHAPTER 5
Writing Creatively with Style

Essays aren't the same as short stories. Novels certainly aren't the same as blogs. And we can't equate songs and memoirs— or can we? Even though every one of these types of creative writing is certainly different from the other, they all share the same quality: *style*. All good writing has its own unique and unmistakable style. In this chapter, you'll discover how to craft your own style in all of your creative writing. This will help you make your words express your heart and soul.

Elements of Style

What is *style* and how do you craft your own individual style in your writing? Let's answer the first part of the question: namely, *an author's style is his or her distinctive way of writing*. A writer's style can be formal or informal, plain or ornate, ironic or allusive, or serious or humorous, to name a few.

Style is made up of many elements, including these:

- diction
- figures of speech
- sentence form and function
- repetition
- rhythm and rhyme
- tone
- voice

Writers may change their style for different kinds of writing and different audiences. In poetry, for example, writers might use more imagery than they would use in prose. This would create a more lush and descriptive style.

> *Prose* is any kind of writing that is not poetry. Essays, novels, and short stories are all examples of prose.

Now to the second part of this question: how do you develop your own writing style? Try these easy and effective methods:

❧ Start by reading through this chapter to become more familiar with the different elements of style.

❧ Study your own creative writing to see which of the stylistic elements described in this chapter you already make part of your writing and how you use them. Think about which ones appeal to you the most.

❧ Jot down the names of some authors whose writing you especially enjoy. Then figure out why you like their writing. For example, you might like the way Stephen King builds suspense or the way Dave Barry uses humor. Think about using these stylistic elements in your own writing. Practice the techniques to see if they feel comfortable to you.

❧ Broaden your horizons by reading writers who are similar to your favorites. If you like John Grisham, try Tom Clancy, Nelson DeMille, Scott Turow, Patricia Cornwell, Robert Ludlum, Michael Crichton, or Mary Higgins Clark, among others. If you prefer memoirs and biographies, check out William Styron, David McCullough, Doris Kearns Goodwin, Tracy Kidder, and Carl Sandburg.

❧ See how each writer handles the elements you like. How do the writers express themselves in dialogue and description, for example?

❧ Traditionally, beginning writers learned style by memorizing long passages written by classic writers. You can update this technique by deciding which stylistic elements from master writers you can use in your own writing. Then practice using these techniques by writing brief passages in the style of your favorite author. After you can create someone else's writing style, you can vary it to suit your own words and ideas.

Now, let's look at some of the different elements of style, starting with *diction*, or word choice.

Using Diction to Create Style

The words you select make up your diction. The words you choose can be short or long, familiar or obscure, formal or informal, technical or ordinary, abstract or concrete, everyday or elevated. For example, how would you describe the diction in the following excerpt from Carson McCullers's short story "The Mortgaged Heart"?

> *To the spectator, the amateur philosopher, no motive among the complex ricochets of our desires and rejections seems stronger or more enduring than the will of the individual to claim his identity and belong. From infancy to death, the human being is obsessed by these dual motives.*

Notice the words *spectator, philosopher, ricochets,* and *obsessed.* These multisyllabic words are elevated and formal. These are words we might find in a university lecture or a textbook. McCullers is using an elevated, formal diction to match her serious subject.

Contrast the Carson McCullers excerpt to these lines from Toni Cade Bambara's short story "Gorilla, My Love":

> *That was the year Hunca Bubba changed his name. Not a change up, but a change back, since Jefferson Winston Vale was the name in the first place. Which was news to me cause he'd been my Hunca Bubba my whole lifetime, since I couldn't manage Uncle to save my life. So far as I was concerned it was a change*

*completely to somethin soundin very geographical weatherlike to
me, like somethin you'd find in an almanac.*

Bambara uses a very informal diction, marked by the words *cause*
(instead of *because*), *somethin* (instead of *something*), and *soundin*
(instead of *sounding*). She is using a type of diction called *dialect*
to show how people speak in a particular region or area. In a
dialect, certain words are spelled and pronounced differently. This
type of diction helps Bambara describe her characters and setting
more fully.

Suit Diction to Your Readers

Which level of diction should you use? It all depends on your
audience, the people who will be reading your words. Knowing
your audience is key to the success of any type of writing, whether
it's poetry or prose. Match your diction to your subject and audience. For example, you'll probably use elevated diction with long,
formal words if you're writing a serious blog entry. You might use
a much simpler diction, perhaps even dialect, if you're writing a
short story.

Sort Out Confusing Word Pairs

Mark Twain once said, "The difference between the right word
and the nearly right word is the same as that between lightning
and the lightning bug." Twain was correct, but sometimes knowing which words are which can be confusing.

That's because English has many similar words that are often
mistaken for one another. Sometimes it's because the words
sound alike; other times it's because the words are spelled alike
but carry different meanings. In either case, distinguishing
between confusing words is important because it helps you
choose the words you need to write exactly what you mean.

> *Homonyms* are words with the same spelling and pro-
> nunciation but different meanings (*lie/lie*), while *homo-
> phones* are words with the same pronunciation but
> different spellings and meanings (*coarse/course*).

To make it easier for you to concentrate on style, I've listed the fifty word pairs and groups that are often confused and therefore misused. Use this list to help you select the exact word you need.

The Fifty Most Often Confused Words

1. *accept:* to receive
   except: to leave out, to exclude

2. *advise:* to guide
   advice: guidance

3. *air:* atmosphere
   err: to make a mistake

4. *affect:* to influence; to assume
   affect: a psychological state
   effect: to cause to come into being; to accomplish
   effect: impact; purpose

5. *a lot:* many
   allot: to divide

6. *altar:* platform upon which religious rites are performed
   alter: to change

7. *allowed:* given permission
   aloud: out loud, verbally

8. *all together:* all at one time
   altogether: completely

9. *already:* previously
   all ready: completely prepared

10. *allusion:* reference to a famous person, place, event,
    work of art, or work of literature
    illusion: misleading appearance; deception

11. *among:* three or more people, places, or things
    between: two people, places, or things

12. *amount:* things that *can't* be counted
    number: things that *can* be counted

13. *are:* plural verb
    our: belonging to us

14. *ascend:* to move up
    assent: to agree

15. *bare:* to uncover
    bare: unadorned, plain, undressed
    bear: animal
    bear: to carry, hold

16. *base:* bottom part of an object; plate in baseball; morally
    low
    bass: lowest male voice; musical instrument
    bass: type of fish

17. *beau:* sweetheart
    bow: to bend into a curve; to play a stringed instrument
    bow: device used to propel arrows; loops of ribbon
    bow: to bend from the waist; to submit
    bow: forward end of a ship
    bough: tree branch

18. *berth:* sleeping area in a ship
    birth: being born

19. *board:* thin piece of wood; group of directors
    bored: uninterested

20. *born:* native, brought forth by birth
    borne: endured (past participle of *to bear*)

21. *bore:* tiresome person
    boar: male pig

22. *brake:* device for slowing a vehicle
    break: to crack or destroy

23. *bread:* baked goods
    bred: reared or born

24. *breadth:* side-to-side dimension
    breath: inhalation and exhalation

25. *buy:* to purchase
    by: near, next to

26. *capital:* official seat of government; highly important;
    business term
    capitol: state government buildings
    Capitol: building in Washington, D.C., where U.S.
    Congress meets

27. *conscience:* moral sense
    conscious: awake

28. *cent:* penny
    scent: aroma

29. *cheep:* what a bird says
    cheap: inexpensive

30. *deer:* animal
    dear: beloved

31. *draft:* breeze
    draft: sketch
    draft: to select for a purpose

32. *dye:* to change color
    die: to cease living

33. *emigrate:* to move away from one's country
    immigrate: to move to another country

34. *eminent:* distinguished
    imminent: expected momentarily
    immanent: inborn, inherent

35. *fare:* price charged for transporting a passenger
    fair: not biased; moderately large; moderately good

36. *gorilla:* ape
    guerrilla: soldier

37. *grate:* irritate; to reduce to small pieces
    grate: frame for stove or fireplace
    great: big, wonderful

38. *hair:* stuff on your head
    heir: beneficiary
    hare: rabbit

39. *here:* in this place
    hear: to listen

40. *hours:* sixty-minute periods
    ours: belonging to us

41. *it's:* contraction for "it is"
    its: possessive pronoun

42. *lay:* to put down
    lie: to be flat

43. *lead:* to conduct
    lead: bluish-gray metal
    led: past tense of *to lead*

44. *loose:* not tight, not fastened; watery; lacking morals
    loose: to untighten, or to let go
    lose: to misplace

45. *peace:* calm
    piece: section

46. *plain:* not beautiful; obvious
    plane: airplane; surface; tool; tree variety

47. *presence:* company, closeness
    presents: gifts

48. *principal:* main; head of a school
    principle: rule

49. *than:* comparison
    then: at that time

50. *their:* belonging to them
they're: contraction for *they are*
there: place

> "A word is not a crystal, transparent and unchanged; it is the skin of a living thought and may vary greatly in color and content according to the circumstances and the time in which it is used."
>
> —Oliver Wendell Holmes

Using Figures of Speech to Create Style

As you read the following passage, describe its style. Then see how the writer creates the effects that you most admire.

> But, soft! what light through yonder window breaks?
> It is the east, and Juliet is the sun.
> Arise, fair sun, and kill the envious moon,
> Who is already sick and pale with grief,
> That thou her maid art far more fair than she:
> Be not her maid, since she is envious;
> Her vestal livery is but sick and green
> And none but fools do wear it; cast it off.
> It is my lady, O, it is my love!
> O, that she knew she were!

In this excerpt from *Romeo and Juliet,* Shakespeare creates beautiful images and feelings of love and longing. He does this by using a number of *figures of speech* (or *figurative language*), words and expressions not meant to be taken literally. Writers use figures of speech to create vivid word pictures, make their writing more emotionally intense, and state their ideas in new and striking ways. As a result, figures of speech appeal to both hearts and minds.

Here are some of the common figures of speech you might want to use in your own writing:

❧ *Apostrophe* The speaker directly addresses an absent person or personified quality, object, or idea. "Arise, fair sun . . ." is an example of apostrophe.

❧ *Similes*   The writer compares two unlike things, the more familiar thing describing the less familiar one. The words *like* or *as* are used to make the comparison.

❧ *Metaphors* A comparison, but without the linking words *like* or *as*. "It is the east, and Juliet is the sun" is a metaphor.

❧ *Personification* The writer gives human traits to non-human things. Shakespeare personifies the sun and moon when he writes: "Arise, fair sun, and kill the envious moon, / Who is already sick and pale with grief . . ." Effective personification of things makes them seem vital and alive, as if they were human.

Try using figures of speech in your creative writing to describe people, places, and things with precision and lyric beauty. This helps you create memorable images that linger in your readers' minds long after they have finished reading your words.

Using Repetition to Create Style

Repetition is using the same sound, word, phrase, line, or grammatical structure over and over deliberately, to link related ideas and emphasize key points. Here's how Charles Dickens used repetition in the famous opening of *A Tale of Two Cities:*

> *It was the best of times, it was the worst of times, it was the age of wisdom, it was the age of foolishness, it was the epoch of belief, it was the epoch of incredulity, it was the season of Light, it was the season of Darkness, it was the spring of hope, it was the winter of despair, we had everything before us, we had nothing before us, we were all going direct to Heaven, we were all going direct the other way—in short, the period was so far like the present period, that some of its noisiest authorities insisted on its being received, for good or for evil, in the superlative degree of comparison only.*

Notice how Dickens begins each sentence with the same phrase, "It was the . . ." Further, Dickens makes his writing style even more interesting by omitting the coordinating conjunction *and* between complete sentences, as in: "It was the best of times, [and] it was the worst of times." Now, you can do the same thing.

> When John F. Kennedy used repetition in his inaugural speech, he created one of most famous lines of the twentieth century: "And so, my fellow Americans, ask not what your country can do for you—ask what you can do for your country."

Repetition, Not Wordiness

Sometimes creative writers confuse repetition with using unnecessary words. Wordy writing forces your readers to clear away unnecessary words and phrases before they can appreciate your style and understand your message. Below are some wordy phrases and their concise cousins. You'll want to use the concise expressions to make your writing powerful.

Wordy	Concise	Wordy	Concise
at the present time	now	in order to	to
at this point in time	now	most unique	unique
complete stop	stop	past history	history
due to the fact that	because	proceed ahead	proceed
few in number	few	revert back	revert
final completion	completion	set a new record	set a record
foreign imports	imports	small in size	small
free gift	gift	true facts	facts
honest truth	truth	weather event	rain (snow, etc.)

> "You become a good writer just as you become a good joiner: by planing down your sentences."
> —Anatole France

Using Sentence Form and Function to Create Style

A *sentence* is a group of words that expresses a complete thought. A sentence has two parts: a *subject* and a *predicate.* The subject includes the noun or pronoun that identifies the subject. The predicate contains the verb that describes what the subject is doing.

Sentence Structure

The structure of a sentence is determined by the number of clauses in the sentence. A clause is a group of words that has a subject and a verb.

❧ An *independent clause* is a complete sentence.

❧ A *dependent clause* is a sentence fragment, a sentence part.

There are four basic types of sentences: *simple sentences, compound sentences, complex sentences,* and *compound-complex sentences.* Let's look at each type of sentence a little more closely to see how you can use them to create your own personal style.

Sentence Type	Definition	Examples
Simple	1 independent clause	I wrote a novel last year. independent clause
Compound	2 or more independent clauses joined by a semicolon or a coordinating conjunction (*and, for, nor, but, or, yet, so*)	I wrote a novel, independent clause but conjunction I prefer writing essays. independent clause
Complex	1 independent clause and 1 or more dependent clauses	When I write fiction, dependent clause I make an outline first. independent clause
Compound-complex	2 or more independent clauses and 1 or more dependent clauses.	If I don't have many chores, dependent clause I write all day long; independent clause but I take a break to jog. independent clause

Sentence Functions

In addition to classifying sentences by the number of clauses they contain, we can describe sentences according to their function. There are four sentence functions in English: *declarative, exclamatory, interrogative,* and *imperative*. Each one has a different style and function.

1. *Declarative sentences* state an idea. They end with a period.

   Example: "The most original authors are not so because they advance what is new, but because they put what they have to say as if it had never been said before."   —Johann Wolfgang von Goethe

2. *Exclamatory sentences* show strong emotions.

   Example: I can't believe I ate the entire box of cookies!

3. *Interrogative sentences* ask a question.

   Example: What project do you plan to write next?

4. *Imperative sentences* give orders or directions, and so end with a period or an exclamation mark.

   Example: Always keep a hard copy of your manuscript, even if you have saved it on your hard drive.

Sentence Style

You can explore writing style by crafting sentences of different lengths and types. You'll probably want to revise your sentences to express your ideas in the best possible way. Here are some ideas to get you started:

❧ Match sentence length and style to your reader's needs and expectations. For example, when your topic is complicated or full of numbers, use simple sentences to make it easier for readers to grasp the main idea.

❧ Always consider your reason for writing before you select a sentence type. For example, if you're trying to show tension and excitement in a story, you'll probably want short, declarative sentences.

❧ Choose the subject of each sentence based on what you want to emphasize. Since readers focus on the subject of your sentence, make it the most important aspect of each thought.

❧ Consider mixing simple, compound, complex, and compound-complex sentences for a more effective style.

❧ Have some fun with sentences. For example, why not try inverting word order to create interesting sentences? Most English sentences follow the subject-verb-direct object pattern, so varying this pattern creates emphasis and interest.

❧ Repeat key words or ideas to achieve emphasis and a more memorable style.

Remember that most effective sentences are concise, conveying their meaning in as few words as possible. Most important of all: don't sacrifice clarity for style. It's not enough that a sentence sounds good; it must also convey its point clearly.

> Keep the subject and verb close together in very long sentences to make the sentences easier to read and understand.

Using Rhythm and Rhyme to Create Style

Rhyme is the repeated use of identical or nearly identical sounds. *End rhyme* occurs when words at the end of lines of poetry have the same sound. For example, lines that end with the words *bat, cat, sat,* or *rat* would have end rhyme. *Internal rhyme* occurs when words within a sentence share the same sound, as in "Each narrow cell in which we dwell." *Cell* and *dwell* have internal rhyme because they share the same sound and one of the words is set in the middle of the line.

Here are a few rhyming lines from Samuel Taylor Coleridge's famous poem *The Rime of the Ancient Mariner.* Notice how *shrink* and *drink* rhyme.

> Water, water, everywhere,
> And all the boards did shrink;
> Water, water, everywhere
> Nor any drop to drink.

Poets and songwriters often use rhyme to create a musical sound, meaning, and structure. It's rare to see rhyme in prose, especially serious prose, such as memoirs, drama, and short stories, but that doesn't mean that prose doesn't have a beat. The language has to flow smoothly.

Rhythm is a pattern of stressed and unstressed syllables that creates a beat, as in music. The *meter* of a poem is its rhythm. Unlike rhyme, all good writing has rhythm—prose as well as poetry. The rhythm reinforces your main idea and makes your words pleasing to the ear. Here are two ways to get rhythm into your writing:

✌ As you write, play music with a strong rhythm to help you give your own words a beat.

✌ After you draft, read you words aloud and listen for the rhythm. Or have a friend read your writing to you. Then adjust the rhythm by adding words, deleting words, choosing new words, or rearranging words.

Using Tone to Create Style

The *tone* of a piece of writing is the author's attitude toward his or her subject matter. For example, the writer's tone can be formal or informal, friendly or distant, personal or pompous. It may be fiery or mellow, bitter or sweet, sad or reassuring, too. How would you describe the tone of the following passage from Thomas Paine's pamphlet *The American Crisis*?

> *These are the times that try men's souls: The summer soldier and the sunshine patriot will in this crisis, shrink from the service of his country; but he that stands it NOW, deserves the love and thanks of man and woman. Tyranny, like hell, is not easily conquered; yet we have this consolation with us, that the harder the*

conflict, the more glorious the triumph. What we obtain too cheap, we esteem too lightly: 'Tis dearness only that gives everything its value.

Paine opens with a reasonable tone but quickly progresses to an incendiary, fiery attitude. He uses this tone to persuade people to support American independence from English rule. Paine's diction ("summer soldier," "sunshine patriot") suggests that some people support you only when it's convenient, but real friends stand by you when the going gets tough.

As you write, choose words that help you convey the tone you want. Are you trying to persuade someone to see things your way? Then you might want emotional words with strong connotations. Are you trying to reassure or soothe someone in a poem or song? Then you'll probably want soft, calm words that put people at ease.

> A word's *connotations* are its emotional overtones. The word *home*, for example, carries the connotations of family, warmth, and love. The word *house*, which has the same meaning, doesn't carry these connotations.

Using Voice to Create Style

Voice is the sense that a real person is behind the flat words on the page. For example, if I've done my job well here, you should get to know me as you read this book. My concern, caring, and competency should come across. You should sense my pride in your attempt to write and my belief that you will succeed as a writer. I'm using my real voice, but there's no rule that says you have to write as yourself.

As a result, the voice you use in your writing can be your own, close to your own, or entirely different. In *Misery*, for instance, Stephen King writes as Paul Sheldon, author of a best-selling series of historical romances. Readers can assume that the voice is fairly close to King's own, as the author of a best-selling series of horror novels.

The following lines from Anne Bradstreet's poem "Upon the Burning of Our House" clearly show her voice is her own. Bradstreet, one of America's earliest settlers, had been burned out of her frontier home.

In silent night when rest I took
For sorrow near I did not look
I wakened was with thund'ring noise
And piteous shrieks of dreadful voice.
The fearful sound of "Fire!" and "Fire!"
Let no man know is my desire.

Can you feel her anguish?

Writers very often adopt a *persona,* or mask, to help them create a voice that is very different from their own personality. For example, poet Ezra Pound wrote as a young Asian girl in his poem "The River-Merchant's Wife: A Letter." Here's a sample stanza:

At fourteen I married My Lord you.
I never laughed, being bashful.
Lowering my head, I looked at the wall.
Called to, a thousand times, I never looked back.

Voice lets you tell stories that are uniquely your own. Getting to know your voice can be a perilous process, because in so doing you are revealing much of yourself. But it's worth the effort because it gives your writing life.

You Must Remember This
An author's style is his or her distinctive way of writing. Use the elements of style—diction, figures of speech, sentence form and function, repetition, rhythm, rhyme, tone, and voice—to help you communicate with your readers with grace and beauty. As E. L. Doctorow said, "Good writing is supposed to evoke sensation in the reader—not the fact that it is raining, but the feeling of being rained upon."

CHAPTER 6
How Blogging Helps You Become a Creative Writer

Here's a snippet from a friend's blog. I'll bet that you find it as emotional as I do:

Wednesday, December 27th

9:13 am   ***Christmas Carol***
Scrooge to Fred's Wife: "And you, my dear . . . would you forgive a stupid old man who doesn't want to be left out in the cold any more?"

Gets me every time.

You've probably heard the term *blog* over and over, because it seems like everyone is blogging. But what is a blog and how can keeping one help you become a more creative writer?

Definition of a Blog

Blog is one of those made-up words created to describe something new. It's actually not a new concept at all, just a new way of sharing your creative writing. A blog is an online diary, a personal record of your ideas that you publish as a Web page. Originally the term was *Weblog*—literally, a Web log. The letters *we* were dropped, and the term was shortened to *blog*. The person who keeps a blog is called a blogger. Blogs became popular in the early 1990s; the term *blog* was coined around 1999.

As with traditional journals, blogs are often updated daily and reflect the writer's personality, ideas, and creativity. The entries are displayed online in reverse chronological order, from most recent to least recent.

So how are blogs different from traditional diaries and journals? First of all, when you blog, you're no longer keeping a journal for yourself. Throw away the lock! Toss out the key! When you blog, you're writing for a wider audience. You have the expectation that others will read it. After all, how many people will ever read your traditional diary? Just a handful, and only if you decide to pass your diary around. In contrast, hundreds, thousands, and even millions of people can read your blog.

Here are some birthday wishes my daughter's friend posted on her blog. More than five hundred people read her blog that day.

My friends are awesome . . .   [Dec. 7th, 2005|**10:37 am**]

I woke up to these:

Sugarplum: happy birthday love! i hope this day is as special and unique as you are! (cheesy, i know, but true)
Auto response from Sugarplum610: HAPPY BIRTHDAY SAMMI!!
i miss you . . . and donuts

Alexjanderam: HAPPY BIRFDAY! HAPPY HAPPY HAPPY HAPPY HAPPY HAPPY BIRFDAY!
Alexjanderam: you old person you.

Xaverrikt: It's your birthday! You're old!!!
Xaverrikt: whoops. typo. ;-)
Xaverrikt: You're 21 years old.
Xaverrikt: Nah.
Xaverrikt: You're still old.
Xaverrikt: *hugs* I hope your day is as fabulous as your penguin icon!

Dina R wrote
happy birthday to the best RA / tuba play in pep band who e-mails

the freshman before in the whole world! :D
-that kinda made no sense... just like me

Alex P wrote
at this point it seems like it would almost be more meaningful to
NOT send you a happy birthday note because that seems to be
what all the cool kids are doing these days. But I just can't help
myself. Happy Bday!
~your co for life~

Jenny B wrote
Happy birthday to one of the sweetest and most genuine people i
know!!! I'm taking you out. Have an amazing day beautiful!!

As you can see, blogs are a great way to share your writing with a
wide audience, to build a fan base, and to become involved with
a community of writers. In effect, when you blog, you are publishing. That's because blogging is online publication. Thanks to
blogs, you no longer need a printing press to share your creative
writing.

> Blogs enable you to keep in touch with people you
> know as well as make new friends.

It's not surprising that blogs are wildly popular. In 2004,
Merriam-Webster anointed *blog* the word of the year. According
to current estimates, more than a *billion* blogs have been posted
and are updated regularly. Established journalism schools and creative writing programs now offer classes in blogging, too.

Some Blogging Terms to Know
The following chart defines some of the blogging terms you will
encounter. I have also included some additional useful terms so
that you can enter the blogging community with more confidence.

Term	Definition
blog	online diary/journal
blogger	person who runs a blog
blogorrhea	excessive or incoherent postings
blog site	Web location (the URL) of the blog
blogsnob	a person who refuses to respond to comments on their blog posted by strangers
blogstorm	a lot of postings on a blog on a specific subject or issue
cyberspace	the realm of electronic communication
plog	a political blog
post	to put an entry on your blog
storyblog	blogs used to publish stories and poetry written by creative writers
troll	a commentator who attacks the views posted on a blog

Why Blog?

Here's an entry from another friend's blog. Does it describe your feelings today?

I love these things . . . [Oct. 3rd|**12:17 am**]
SAGITTARIUS (NOV. 22- DEC.21): Sit down with a pen or pencil. This might be a good week to write down your goals or to put your inspirations into words. Let your inner poet have a chance to shine.

As a creative writer, there are many reasons why you should consider blogging. Here are some of the most persuasive ones:

Spark Your Creativity

Blogs are a great way to share your writing. Since blogs are informal, you can be more casual about polishing your writing. A blog allows you to be wildly original and inventive because you can write whatever you want—as long as you don't slander or defame anyone, of course. And blogs can be great wellsprings of inspiration, serving as your own personal idea books.

Further, because readers can leave comments on your postings, you can have online conversations with your readers. This can be another great spark to your creativity as you bounce ideas off other people. These comments help you develop your ideas because you're getting feedback.

Write More Easily

Let's return to my comment about blogs being "informal." Since a blog is your own personal journal, you don't have the pressure you would have writing for a class or a traditional publication. No one is standing over you with a red pen, after all. When you blog, you do want to follow the rules of standard written English, but there's not the pressure to be absolutely correct in all spelling, punctuation, and grammar issues. This helps make blogging fun, since the pressure is off as you share your ideas and imagination with others in writing. We all know that writing can be lonely, difficult work. By becoming part of a community of writers, you're no longer alone. This helps take the drudgery out of creative writing.

Polish Your Writing Skills

Blogging can make you a more accomplished and skilled writer because blogging encourages you to write, which is especially important when you're just starting out as a creative writer. The more entries you post to your blog, the more often you're writing. And we all know that practice makes perfect. In addition, you get feedback from interested readers, which can help you polish your writing skills even more.

Establish a Platform

Blogs can be very effective methods of self-promotion and marketing. By blogging, you can attract an audience of interested readers, which is called establishing a *platform* in the publishing business. You might be able to parlay your fame as a blogger into a book contract if that is your goal.

Influence Public Opinion

Last but not least, blogs empower everyday people with the ability to broadcast their opinions on news, sports, finance—anything that interests them—to the entire world. Information and comments posted on blogs can even influence major events, including elections. Through your writing, blogs give you the power to become a maker and shaper of public opinion, or the opportunity just to weigh in on issues that matter to you. As a blogger, you have the ability to raise awareness of important issues. As a result, your writing can provide a valuable, even invaluable, public service.

Be a Responsible Blogger

Writers have always had tremendous power. For instance, Harriet Beecher Stowe's 1852 novel *Uncle Tom's Cabin* was the most influential book of the nineteenth century. The suffering of the fictional slaves Eliza and Uncle Tom touched many people otherwise unmoved by the cold rhetoric of the abolitionists. The novel's message is clear: slavery is evil, but the evil is in slavery itself, not the South. Stowe urged white Northerners to welcome escaped slaves and to treat them with respect. Despite its stereotypical characters, convoluted plot, and stilted writing, the novel so inflamed the nation that when Stowe met Abraham Lincoln during the Civil War, he said, "So this is the little lady who made this big war!"

But with great power comes great responsibility. The digital frontier is still wild and woolly. Amid the excitement of being part of a worldwide community of writers and political gurus, ethical lines can get blurred. To further complicate the issue, people who generate blog content are making up the rules as they go along because nothing has yet been firmly established and cyberspace is not policed. If you decide to use your blog as a political forum for your creative writing, consider these guidelines:

- ❧ *Don't post unverified information.* It's always difficult to balance the public's right to know with your right to express your opinions. Your responsibility is to verify all the information that you share, so be sure that you can verify everything you post on your blog. You don't want to be responsible for passing on information that's not true.

❧ *Don't inflate yourself and your accomplishments.* You wouldn't do it on your résumé, so don't do it in cyberspace. For example, if you have spoken to a publisher about submitting a manuscript, don't post "I have a book deal with a major publisher." You don't; you've merely had a conversation about a possible submission.

❧ *Be careful about venting and ranting.* Conventional print journals are great places to release tension through writing, but remember that the comments you post on your blog are open for everyone to read. We all have frustrating days, but when you post your dissatisfactions on your blog, people may get the wrong impression of you. Some blogs have restricted spaces, open only to the people you designate. Nonetheless, there's nothing to stop those readers from passing around your postings, intentionally or not.

❧ *Don't slur anyone, least of all your employer.* So many people have lost their jobs as a result of information they've posted on their blogs that there's even a special term for getting fired for this: *dooced*. The word came from Heather Armstrong's blog pseudonym. She lost her job after writing satirical accounts of her workplace on her personal blog.

❧ *Don't assume you can hide behind a fake name.* Many writers assume pseudonyms when they blog (just as traditional writers have done for centuries), but even a fake name is no protection against people figuring out who you are.

> Remember that nothing you post on your blog is ever private, no matter how you restrict it. Once your writing is in cyberspace, it's there for everyone to read.

How to Blog

Here's part of a blog entry from Katie Greenberger, posted while she was studying in Cairo for a year. As you read it, decide what techniques Katie uses to make her writing so interesting.

Monday, October 09
In Which She Mangles a Pomegranate

It's pomegranate season. Mangos are still out in force, as are dates (though they now come mainly in dried form for Ramadan, you can still find a ton of the bright red sugary ones), but my personal favorite—the fresh fig—has been retired. Thus, I have been trying a number of different fruits in an attempt to make up for the lack of fig-age. Past experiments have included the suddenly super-delicious pear (they're actually *crunchy* here) and the incredibly questionable caca, a fruit that resembles a tomato past its prime. My roommate insists caca is wonderful. Erin and I beg to differ.

Today's experiment was the pomegranate. First, I need to note how unbelievably amazing the pomegranate is. It's sweet and crunchy and tart and somehow satisfies whatever it is you need. However, the pomegranate will not lie down and submit to consumption the way a banana or apple will. No, the pomegranate insists on going out William Wallace-style, shrieking "Freeeeeeeeeeeeeeeeeedom!" as it spritzes purple juice everywhere. Said purple juice will not come out in the wash, a final reminder never to mess with the pomegranate again. It took me over half an hour to eat exactly half of the 840 seeds every pomegranate possesses. About.com tells me I went about this all the wrong way, but I first cut the pomegranate in half and then proceeded to mash the pomegranate into submission with my fingers, hacking and tearing away at the incredibly tough rind. This merely produced more juice than fruit for my efforts. Using a knife to entice the seeds out didn't really work either. I resorted to picking the seeds out one by one, which may have had something to do with why I spent over half an hour on a fruit. Sorry, half a fruit. Half a delicious fruit of great nutritional merit, but half an hour nonetheless. Pomegranates are not the kind of food one wants when one is hungry.

Do not mess with a pomegranate, for they are apparently a good deal wiser than I am. They also apparently can go up to three months in a fridge, so I may bide my time before engaging the second pomegranate in a rematch. I'll be ready for it, though.
POSTED BY KT AT **3:32 PM**

Katie has a flair for using specific sensory details, which enables her to make even everyday events—such as eating a piece of fruit—fascinating to read. She made me want to stop writing, run right out, and buy a pomegranate . . . and I don't even like them.

Here are some things you can post to your blog:

❧ Snippets of ideas that have touched your heart strings, as shown in the entry that I used in the opening of this chapter. These bits and pieces can be movie quotes, newspaper stories, comments from friends, and so on.

❧ Intriguing information that you want to share with your audience, such as the horoscope you just read, news about your pet lizard, the tulips poking up in your garden on a frosty April morning, or how you waxed your legs.

❧ Descriptions of everyday events in your life. Katie used this technique in the entry that you just read.

❧ Commentary on a particular subject. Common subjects include current events, politics, and gossip. One of the most widely read blog commentaries is the *Drudge Report*, established by the reporter Matt Drudge.

❧ News stories. Many reporters maintain their own blogs. Some blogs can become important sources of news, as we saw during the tsunami tragedy of December 2004. During that time, Doctors Without Borders used blogs to send reports from affected areas in Sri Lanka and southern India. The same thing happened during and directly after Hurricane Katrina in August 2005. On-site bloggers sent out news reports before the traditional print media was able to get reporters into the region.

❧ Passages from your own creative writing in progress. You can post part or all of a short story, for instance, and have your readers comment on it. You can then use these comments as the basis for you revisions.

❧ Opinions. While campaigning or thinking of campaigning, politicians now often maintain blogs to form bonds with voters. Marketing and public relations firms often have blogs now. You can share your opinions as well.

❧ Images. Blogs often contain photographs and pictures to illustrate the words. These visuals make blog entries more interesting and descriptive.

As you can tell from this list, a blog can be posted by one person, a group of people, or by a business.

You can easily set up your blog on a blog hosting service or run your blog with special software designed for that purpose. Just look up "blog hosting service" or "blog software" on the Internet to find specific information. Many of these services are free, too, so it won't cost you anything to establish and maintain your own blog.

Ways to Get People to Read Your Blog

If you decide to post a blog, it's probably because you want to share your creative writing. Of course, it's not enough just to post blog entries—you also have to attract an audience, just as you would with a print publication. Here are some easy and effective ways to build your online community:

Give Your Blog a Good Name and Description

You know that first impressions matter. Just as you would take the time to craft a brilliant title for your short story, novel, poem, or essay, so you must take the time to give your blog an effective title and description. Your title should accomplish two purposes: suggest the contents of your blog and make your audience want to read it.

Here's the title and subheading for my blog:

TEST SUCCESS: GRAMMAR, SHE WROTE

HI! I'M DR. LAURIE ROZAKIS, A PROFESSOR OF ENGLISH, AUTHOR OF MORE THAN 100 BOOKS, AND A NATIONALLY RECOGNIZED EXPERT AT HELPING PEOPLE MASTER THE GRAMMAR, WRITING, AND TEST-TAKING SKILLS THEY NEED TO SUCCEED. CHECK MY BLOG AND SEND ME YOUR QUESTIONS ON GRAMMAR, WRITING, AND TEST-TAKING.

---

http://rozakile.blogspot.com/index.html

Here's the title and subheading of Katie Greenberger's blog:

CairoKate: Insh'allah and All That Jazz

A GLOBE-TROTTER SHARES HER THOUGHTS—WHETHER OR NOT THEY HAVE ANYTHING TO DO WITH GLOBE-TROTTING IS COMPLETELY IRRELEVENT. KNITTING, DANCING, EGYPT, POLITICS, ARABIC, MUSIC, THE TRIALS AND TRIBULATIONS OF BEING A YOUNG AMERICAN.

Notice how both examples attract your attention and make you want to read on. The writers accomplish this with specific details and descriptions.

Make Your Blog Attractive

That's easy to do because most blog programs have beautiful templates that you can use. Include pictures, visuals, and other graphics to make your pages pretty. Notice in the two previous examples how the writers used different fonts (typefaces) to make the headings attractive.

Post Often

To attract an audience, try to post at least every other day. If you only post every few weeks, you're less likely to attract an audience.

Make Your Entries Interesting

Here's one of the basic guidelines of creative writing: if you write about something that you find interesting and feel passionate about, chances are good that your audience will catch your enthusiasm.

Below is an entry my son made on his blog that I found interesting because of his use of vivid words and specific details.

10:52 am ***Not dead***

> Yeah, I know, I blitzed like crazy for two weeks, and then nothing for almost a week. Blame New Year's traveling, renewed busyness at work, and the fact that Rebecca is back from vacation. Of course, I'm going to Puerto Rico for the next four days, so don't expect to hear much from me until next week.
>
> That said, I promised to talk about my family's New Year's tradition, which we made up ourselves. Each member of my nuclear family gets to pick two foods that they would like for the New Years Day dinner. These foods can be anything you want, healthy or [usually] not, homemade or not. If other people like them, we get enough to share, but you don't have to choose foods with that in mind. And it doesn't matter if anything matches or usually goes together: One year, we had seven fried foods and a chocolate cake.
>
> This year, however, things worked out nicely. I picked crab legs and steak. My father picked onion rings and fruit salad. My sister went for a homemade milkshake and browned-butter spaghetti. And my mother had a chocolate cheesecake and figs. (Don't ask about the figs.) Bonus vegetables made their way to the table, but no one actually ate them.
>
> Mmmm . . . talking about all of this has made me hungry . . .
>
> (5 Comments |**Comment on this**)

Here are some of the words and details that make this writing vibrant:

Effective Words and Phrases	Effective Details
blitzed	These foods can be anything you want, healthy or [usually] not, homemade or not.
nuclear family	One year, we had seven fried foods and a chocolate cake.
went for	I picked crab legs and steak.
browned-butter	My father picked onion rings and fruit salad.
bonus vegetables	My sister went for a homemade milkshake and browned-butter spaghetti.
mmmm . . .	(Don't ask about the figs.)

Keep Your Entries Short

You don't have to post a lot—just a paragraph or two will do. Of course, you can write as much as you want, but you don't have to. Make blogging fun, rather than a chore.

Make Your Entries Easy to Read

Be considerate to your readers. Many people who scan your blog also read many other blogs, so make your entries easy to read. Also remember that reading something on the Web isn't the same as reading a print text. Web readers are used to short, snappy blocks of copy rather than long passages.

Link to Other Sites

Support your entries with links to other relevant blogs and Web sites. This also helps you build a community of readers. In addition, be sure to give credit to other sites that you refer to.

Edit Your Writing
Blogs are informal, but that's no excuse for not checking your writing. Cut out things you say twice or information that strays from the topic. Proofread for grammatical errors. Run the spell-checker.

Be Passionate About Your Writing.
As with any kind of creative writing, blogging works best when you feel strongly about your subject. Tap your emotions and your creativity to create memorable writing, just as you would when you're writing for the print media.

Below is an entry by Bob Greenberger that shows his emotions about the topic and his reasons for posting:

March 29, 2007
David Honigsberg
I'm late with this because I've been out of town, but I do want to acknowledge the passing of my friend, David Honigsberg.

David was a rabbi . . . He did not have a congregation and didn't seem to desire one. Still, I would see him most Wednesdays as part of a circle of friends and when I heard of his death, I realized our circle *was* his congregation. Without his friendship, loyalty and guidance, we are all the poorer for it.

While he and I were part of the circle, we weren't especially close, not as close as some of the other relationships were. Still, when I got the call Tuesday morning that his second heart attack in less than a year claimed his life, I was stunned and saddened. David was too good a friend, too loyal a member of his faith for his passing to make any sense at all. (There's also the pesky fact that we're the same age and you took one look at him, you'd never peg him as the candidate for heart disease.)

The outpouring of commentary on blogs, websites and in private e-mail lists, shows how his absence has begun to diminish us all. . . . I just want to thank David for being a friend, for being someone to chat with and someone who performed acoustic music I enjoyed hearing. I'll miss him and hope he is at rest.

Posted by Bob Greenberger at **07:16 PM** | **Comments (1)** |

You Must Remember This

Starting and maintaining a blog can help you become a more creative writer. Blogging can also help you write more easily, polish your writing skills, become known as a writer, and even influence your readers. Best of all, blogging can be fun!

CHAPTER 7
Writing Creative Essays

What do Sir Francis Bacon (1561–1626), Albert Camus (1913–60), Joan Didion (b. 1934), Ralph Waldo Emerson (1803–82), Mary McCarthy (1912–89), and Joyce Carol Oates (b. 1938) have in common? How about George Orwell (1903–50), Katherine Anne Porter (1890–1980), and Erma Bombeck (1927–96)? Let's add David Sedaris (b. 1956), Susan Sontag (1933–2004), and Virginia Woolf (1882–1941) to the party as well.

On the surface, you probably couldn't assemble a more dissimilar group of people: male and female, serious and humorous, long dead and still very much alive. They hail from the four corners of the globe, too. They're liberal and conservative, rich and poor, contemporary and dusty. So what do all these people have in common? They all wrote brilliant essays. Now you can, too.

As you'll learn in this chapter, essays are one of the ideal ways to express your creativity in writing. That's because essays are brief, personal, and pithy. As a result, they allow you tremendous freedom of expression. They're one of the most elastic forms of creative writing.

> Erma Bombeck's hysterically funny essays described her life as a homemaker. Bombeck was paid just three dollars each for her first essays, but they soon catapulted her to fame and fortune as they were featured in more than seven hundred daily newspapers around the country. She later republished her essays in many best-selling

books. Here's one of my favorite Bombeck quotes: "My second favorite household chore is ironing. My first one is hitting my head on the top bunk bed until I faint."

You're Never Too Busy to Write an Essay

The essayists who opened this chapter are all professional writers, but essay writing is far from restricted to the professionals. You would be astonished to learn how many people in "everyday" occupations have published essays. Anyone can write an essay because the form is so flexible. In addition, writing an essay is not the huge commitment that writing a novel, play, or biography is.

"I'm too busy to write an essay!" you say. "I have a full-time job, a home, children, and a social life." I guarantee that you can find time to write an essay. For example, Dr. Atul Gawande, a noted surgeon, began contributing essays to the online magazine *Slate* when he was just starting his medical career. "I did 30 columns for them, and it was like doing 30 gallbladders," he said. Then he expanded on the form to write four-thousand-to-eight-thousand-word essays for *The New Yorker*. Not surprisingly, Dr. Gawande's writing had turned his life around. In a *New York Times* review he said, "I now feel like writing is the most important thing I do." (April 3, 2007)

You may find that writing essays is the perfect way to unleash your creativity, too.

What is an Essay?

An *essay* is a brief work of writing that treats a topic from the writer's own perspective. As you learned in chapter 2, the term comes from the French word *essayer,* "to try, to attempt." Literally, then, an essay is an attempt to write about a specific topic from your personal point of view.

Essays are

❧ *Nonfiction:* they deal with real life.

❧ *Subjective:* they present the writer's opinion.

❧ *Expository:* they show, tell, or prove in writing.

❧ *Narrative:* they often incorporate stories to convey the writer's point of view.

One of the essay's greatest strengths is its wide variety. So many different kinds of creative writing can be considered essays! Here are a few:

articles	political manifestos
brief autobiographical writing	scientific observations
criticism, such as literary or	short memoirs
social commentary	written comments on
humorous pieces	daily life

Aldous Huxley, himself an essayist, said: "Like the novel, the essay is a literary device for saying almost everything about almost anything. By tradition, almost by definition, the essay is a short piece, and it is therefore impossible to give all things full play within the limits of a single essay. But a collection of essays can cover almost as much ground, and cover it almost as thoroughly, as can a long novel."

> Michel de Montaigne (1533–92) has the distinction of being the first person to name and describe the essay, but Francis Bacon was the first to describe his short writings as essays.

Types of Essays

Let's take a look at the four main types of essays. Then you can decide which ones you would like to write. Here's hoping that you try your hand at all of them.

Persuasive Essays

Just as the title suggests, writers of persuasive essays use words to move the audience to action or belief. Writers can appeal to reason, emotion, their good reputation, or all three. No matter which appeal the writer choses, persuasive essays are most successful when writers support their opinion with specific details and examples.

Below is an excerpt from George Orwell's famous 1946 essay "Politics and the English Language." Orwell tries to convince readers that the English language has deteriorated, becoming both the cause and result of lazy thinking and deceitful and corrupt politics. To convince us, he gives specific examples. As you read this passage, look for the examples. Decide if Orwell convinces you that people should write clear, direct English.

> *Meanwhile, here are five specimens of the English language as it is now habitually written. These five passages have not been picked out because they are especially bad—I could have quoted far worse if I had chosen—but because they illustrate various of the mental vices from which we now suffer. . . .*
>
> *2. Above all, we cannot play ducks and drakes with a native battery of idioms which prescribes egregious collocations of vocables as the Basic put up with for tolerate, or put at a loss for bewilder. Professor Lancelot Hogben (Interglossa)*
>
> *3. On the one side we have the free personality: by definition it is not neurotic, for it has neither conflict nor dream. Its desires, such as they are, are transparent, for they are just what institutional approval keeps in the forefront of consciousness; another institutional pattern would alter their number and intensity; there is little in them that is natural, irreducible, or culturally dangerous. . . . Essay on psychology in Politics (New York)*
>
> *Each of these passages has faults of its own, but, quite apart from avoidable ugliness, two qualities are common to all of them. The first is staleness of imagery; the other is lack of precision. The writer either has a meaning and cannot express it, or he inadvertently says something else, or he is almost indifferent as to whether his words mean anything or not. . . .*

Figures of speech are also called figurative language. No matter what you call this imaginative use of language, a fresh and creative figure of speech is the mark of a skilled writer.

Descriptive Essays

Description is a word picture of what something or someone is like. Description is made up of sensory details that help readers form pictures in their minds. In descriptive essays, writers use the five senses to provide a vivid verbal picture of a person, place, thing, event, or idea.

When you write your descriptive essays, be sure to use figures of speech as well as words that appeal to smell, sight, sound, taste, and touch. Recall that figures of speech are words and expressions that use language in fresh and exciting ways. You have many different figures of speech at your disposal. Here are some of the most common ones:

Figure of Speech	Definition	Example
alliteration	The repetition of initial consonant sounds in several words in a sentence or line of poetry. Use alliteration in your essays to link related ideas and emphasize key words.	About the lilting house and happy as the grass was green
allusion	A reference to a well-known place, event, person, work of art, or other work of literature.	He's caught in a real Catch-22 situation.
hyperbole	Overstating an idea to achieve a specific literary effect.	I'm so hungry I could eat a house!
irony	When something happens that is different from what was expected.	"Was he free? Was he happy? The question is absurd; / Had anything been wrong, we should certainly have heard." —W. H. Auden
metaphor	A comparison between two unlike things; the more familiar thing helps describe the less familiar one.	My heart is a singing bird.

onomatopoeia	The use of words to imitate the sounds they describe. Use onomatopoeia in your descriptive essays to create a smooth style and to reinforce meaning.	crack, hiss, buzz
oxymoron	A seeming contradiction.	living death jumbo shrimp
personification	Giving human traits to nonhuman things.	The wind whistled in the trees.
simile	A figure of speech that compares two unlike things (using *like, as, than,* or *seems* to make the comparison).	"What happens to a dream deferred? Does it dry up like a raisin in the sun?" —Langston Hughes

> Most people think that figures of speech are reserved for poetry alone. Not true! In fact, figures of speech are used in prose (nonpoetry) as much as in poetry.

The following excerpt is from Charles Lamb's famous descriptive essay "A Dissertation on a Roast Pig." As you read it, look for the vivid sensory descriptions and figures of speech. I'll bet your mouth will be watering by the end.

There is no flavor comparable, I will contend, to that of the crisp, tawny, well-watched, not over-roasted, crackling, as it is well called—the very teeth are invited to their share of the pleasure at this banquet in overcoming the coy, brittle resistance—with the adhesive oleaginous—O call it not fat—but an indefinable sweetness growing up to it—the tender blossoming of fat—fat cropped in the bud—taken in the shoot—in the first innocence—the cream and quintessence of the child-pig's yet pure food—the lean, no lean, but a kind of animal manna—or, rather, fat and lean (if it must be so) so blended and running into each other, that both together make but one ambrosian result, or common substance.

Narrative Essays

In these essays, writers tell a story. Unlike short stories, however, narrative essays are nonfiction. They use the elements of a short story—characters, setting, dialogue, theme, point of view, and plot—but the events are real. In most cases, the writer uses the first-person point of view, relating events from his or her own eyes. The narrative can be serious or humorous, just as with any other type of narrative.

For example, in a humorous essay entitled "Taming the Bicycle," Mark Twain tells the story of how he learned to ride a bicycle. The type of bicycle that he learned to ride—the high-wheel bikes of the 1880s—is long obsolete, but Twain's skill at telling a story is eternal. As you read this excerpt, trace the story he tells.

Mine was not a full-grown bicycle, but only a colt—a fifty-inch, with the pedals shortened up to forty-eight—and skittish, like any other colt. The Expert explained the thing's points briefly, then he got on its back and rode around a little, to show me how easy it was to do. He said that the dismounting was perhaps the hardest thing to learn, and so we would leave that to the last. But he was in error there. He found, to his surprise and joy, that all that he needed to do was to get me on to the machine and stand out of the way; I could get off, myself. Although I was wholly inexperienced, I dismounted in the best time on record. He was on that side, shoving up the machine; we all came down with a crash, he at the bottom, I next, and the machine on top.

We examined the machine, but it was not in the least injured. This was hardly believable. Yet the Expert assured me that it was true; in fact, the examination proved it. I was partly to realize, then, how admirably these things are constructed. We applied some Pond's Extract, and resumed. The Expert got on the OTHER side to shove up this time, but I dismounted on that side; so the result was as before.

Expository Essays

As with any other expository writing, expository essays explain, show, or tell. You can remember this because both *expository* and *explain* start with *exp*. Expository essays can be developed in many ways. Here are some of the most useful methods to try:

Type of Expository Development	Explanation
Compare and Contrast	Show how two people, places, or things are the same (compare) and different (contrast).
Examples	State the main idea and back it up with specific instances and proof.
Divide and Classify	Separate items from one another (divide) and group similar things together (classify).
Definition	Define the whole by naming its parts, define something by tracing its origins, give synonyms for the object, or list characteristics of the thing.
Process Analysis	Show how to do something.
Cause and Effect	Show why something happened (the cause) and the result (the effect).

Below is an excerpt from a political essay titled " 'Til the Next Political Alliance Do We Part," written by a brilliant student named Elisabeth Fink. As you read it, analyze the method of development.

Women in the Medieval Ages rarely experienced the full freedom of mobility—both political and otherwise—that men in those times appeared to enjoy. A woman was tied first to her father's fate and then to her husband's. What is intriguing, however, was how upper-class women both were extremely socially limited in their power and, at the same time, able to derive extraordinary influence and importance from marriage and even more so from motherhood. The upper class had the luxury of taking their women and politely stuffing them in a tower of etiquette. A woman's lands were subject to be acquired by her husband and, as Eleanor of Aquitaine proved, her very person was also subject to the whims of her husband. However, a woman of noble birth could be very skilled in the art of political manipulation, like Eleanor, and could control courts from behind the scenes, particularly through her sons, or, if she chose, she could engage in courtly love and could control the man who worshipped the ground on which she walked. Most of the overt influence exerted by medieval women was through the troubadours in Eleanor's Court of Love in Poitiers. However, in order to have any sense of power, an ordinary upper-class woman had to be at the very least married to participate in the courtly love or bear sons in order to be able to engage in politics.

You just read that there are many different kinds of essays, which means that you're sure to find one or more essay pattern to your taste. I suggest that you try writing different varieties, matching each one to your message, mood, and audience. See which essay pattern best fits your unique voice.

How to Write a Creative Essay

You can write an essay any way you wish, of course, but many writers find they can be most creative when they have a plan. Below is the method that I've always used with success. I'm sure that it will help you as well; just follow these easy steps:

- ❧ *Choose your audience.* Who will read your essay? You can't write a single word until you pinpoint your audience. That's because your readers determine every element in your essay, including your level of language, structure, and topic.

- ❧ *Develop a topic.* Find something that interests you as well as your audience. Remember: if you feel passionate about a subject, your enthusiasm will fire up your readers as well.

❧ *Decide the type of essay to write.* Use your audience and topic to determine whether you are going to write a persuasive, descriptive, narrative, or expository essay. Feel free to combine two or more structures; for instance, a narrative essay always has some description. Likewise, a persuasive essay may use a narrative "hook" to grab the reader's attention.

❧ *Pick an essay structure.* Once you know whether you're writing a persuasive, descriptive, narrative, or expository essay, focus on the structure. For example, if you are writing an expository essay, do you want to develop your ideas through examples or compare and contrast structure? In addition, decide how long your essay will be. You might write five hundred to a thousand words, for instance.

❧ *Draft.* You can do some brainstorming and outlining, of course, or just start writing. Regardless of the method you choose to prime the creative pump, this is the time to get your ideas down on paper.

❧ *Revise and polish.* Let your draft sit a few hours or even a few days to "cool off." Then take a look at it with a critical eye. Where can you tighten up your ideas? What new information needs to be added to make your point clear? What makes your essay interesting to read? How can you make it even more compelling?

I know that these seem like a lot of steps, but you'll find that many of these decisions fall into place naturally because some topics are better suited to some methods of development than others.

Write Now

There's no time like the present to let your creativity flow. And aren't you just itching to put into practice all that you've read? Here are some topics that lend themselves to essays. Choose one of these topics, revise it to suit your feelings, or develop your own topic. Try writing more than one essay.

1. Are arranged marriages more successful than love matches? Why or why not?
2. Describe your hero.
3. If you knew that you had only six months to live, how would you spend your time?
4. Describe a skill you've learned or are currently learning.
5. Persuade someone to move to your town.
6. How does your private self differ from your public image?
7. Are dogs or cats better pets?
8. What does it mean to be "educated"? Describe the qualities of a good education.
9. Describe your favorite food. Make your readers hungry for it.
10. What is creativity?
11. Do sports help develop character? Explain.
12. Childhood: joy or misery?

> Erma Bombeck said: "When I stand before God at the end of my life, I would hope that I would not have a single bit of talent left, and could say, 'I used everything you gave me.'" Not a bad way to look at creative writing, eh?

You Must Remember This

An essay is a brief nonfiction writing on a topic of your choice. Essays are personal, presenting your point of view on the topic. They can explain, persuade, tell a story, or describe the topic. They are an ideal form for releasing your inner creativity because they are so flexible.

CHAPTER 8
Memoirs: Your Life Story

———— ∞∞∞ ————

When my first child was born, I started writing my memoirs. So what if I was not yet thirty years old? So what if I was up to my elbows in baby stuff? I knew that my child would eventually want to know about my life—and more. As a result, I included stories not only about my own childhood among Long Island's potato and duck farms, but also stories from my parents, siblings, and in-laws. Here's an excerpt from the oral history I took from my father-in-law, Nick Rozakis, who was born March 9, 1915:

> *I entered the Navy on May 8, 1943, and served until April 1, 1946. Since I was stationed in Chicago for the duration of the war, I tell everyone I successfully protected Lake Michigan from invasion, but I was really a fireman, a specialist F-3rd class. This isn't what I wanted to do at all, so I let a buddy talk me into taking the EDDY test for radio technician. I passed the test, but I flunked out of radio school in three weeks. I really wanted to write, so I applied to* Stars and Stripes. *My application was approved (maybe because I said I was editor-in-chief of the high school newspaper, which wasn't true), but when I went for the interview they discovered I was a fireman so they said, "No writing for you!" Instead, I was sent to be an instructor in firefighters' school. This was the first time I got in trouble . . . but not the last.*

Your memories are like the squares of a beautiful and unique quilt, stitched with love and care. How long have you promised yourself or your family that you would write your memoirs? Let me help you get started.

The Importance of Writing Your Life's Story

I believe that everyone has a unique life story to share. When you put your story down in writing, you enhance everyone's life. This is true not only for the writer, but also for those who have the privilege of reading your memoirs.

Why not just tell your recollections to friends? After all, during the great treks west in the nineteenth century, pioneers and cowboys used to huddle around the campfires and swap life stories. Before television, movies, and the Internet were invented, families sat around the hearth on cold winter nights recounting family stories. And what happened to all those stories? Unless they were written down, they are now lost to us.

Precious Memories

As much fun as it is to recount your life story to family and friends, the stories will be half forgotten or lost altogether if you don't write them down. When you write the story of your life, you create invaluable literary documents. (Winston Churchill once wrote, "History shall be kind to me, for I intend to write it." And so he did.) Your life story goes from temporary to permanent. Your memoirs are important because they

1. conserve the people, places, and events of the past in a unique way;
2. entertain and amuse readers;
3. link the generations in a special way;
4. offer reassurance to your descendants;
5. warn others about dangers they may face, especially concerning medical issues;
6. identify family members and close friends;
7. celebrate your family and its accomplishments;
8. set the record straight on important family issues;
9. often inspire other family members to preserve their own memories;
10. are a priceless historical document.

An Invaluable Legacy

Writing your memoirs means celebrating individual lives, experiences, and relationships. It means preserving joyous and treasured memories as well as passing on the hard-earned lessons and challenges you have faced. Writing your memoirs also serves to unite your entire community as well as your individual family. How is this possible? It's because your memoirs become an historical document, a primary source. Centuries hence, scholars may be reading your memoirs to learn about life in the twentieth and twenty-first centuries. How's that for immortality?

In addition, creative writing is a way of exploring the what and the why of life and making sense of it. As a result, writing a memoir often leads to dramatic insights and personal growth.

Whether the audience is just you, your family members, coworkers, or the world at large, your story deserves to be told. Now that I've persuaded you to invest a little time in a writing project that promises a rich reward, let's get started!

What Is a Memoir?

Before we go any further, what exactly is a memoir? The word *memoir* comes from the Latin word *memoria,* meaning "memory." As you can deduce from the word's history, a memoir is a type of autobiography, the story of a person's life written by the person himself or herself. A memoir is thus based on your own personal experience.

However, memoirs are often far less formal than autobiographies, as they usually do not recount an entire life. As you would expect, most memoirs are told from the first-person point of view, using the pronouns *I* and *me.* Describing his memoir *Palimpsest,* Gore Vidal said: "A memoir is how one remembers one's own life, while an autobiography is history, requiring research, dates, facts double-checked."

A Slice of Life May Suffice

Therefore, a memoir is your memory of part of your life, not your entire life. As a result, you can tell as little or as much as you want, rather than having to cover your entire life from birth on. You don't have to tell it all, so the pressure is off.

Further, since you're writing about events from your life the way that you want, you can include or exclude whatever details you choose. *You* make the rules and you can change them as you go along. Different writers have defined the scope of their memoirs in many different ways. Here are three methods to consider:

❧ Choose a defining moment in your life, a key event that helped establish the entire path your life has taken. In my case, it was my family's move to Long Island when I was nine years old. That move established my lifelong friends, choice of college, and even choice of a career. You might want to describe an illness, the birth of a sibling, your parents' divorce, your first job, or the day you pitched a no-hitter. Perhaps you will want to write about a memorable conversation, meeting, or encounter. The choice is completely yours.

❧ Focus on a year in your life. Describe just that year, looking forward and backward in your life for details that explain why the year was pivotal.

❧ Tell your complete life story, including information about all the major events in your life. If you decide to describe your entire life to date, you'll probably want to use chronological order. This is the order of time. When you write a memoir in chronological order, you start by describing your early childhood, progress to your teen years, and move into your adult experiences.

But the scope of your memoir is completely your decision, so don't feel pressured to tell more or less than you want.

Ways to Gather Memories for Your Memoir

I teach memoir writing, and the most common question I get is, "What do I do first?" There are many different ways to approach this type of creative writing. My students and I have used the following methods with great success:

❧ Draw. You can make a schematic of your house or a map of your town as it looked when you were a child. You can draw your elementary or high school building, the family farm, the barracks where you had basic training, your camping trailer, the local shopping mall. Don't worry if you're not a skilled artist; remember that the drawings serve only to help you remember key details to use in your writing.

❧ List your favorite belongings, now and the past. Include things you've collected over the years, especially the objects you wish you'd never given away. Then jot down notes explaining why each object is important and memorable.

❧ Recall your earliest memories. Interview older relatives and close family friends to see how your memories match theirs. If you're fortunate to still have living parents, grandparents, or aunts and uncles, talk to them. You'll be delighted at the stories they'll recall of your childhood.

❧ You can verify everyone's memories by doing some research in newspapers and magazines written when you were a child. You probably never saw these materials before because you were too young at the time to read. As a result, reading the newspapers from your childhood can help illuminate and clarify events you only dimly remember or understand. They can also help you resolve discrepancies between your memories and those of your relatives and friends.

❧ You may wish to start with one of the highlights of your life, such as a memorable day, a close call, a key childhood memory, a challenge you met with assurance. Most people find that the highlights of their life are almost never the splashy seconds in time (like the day I met John Lennon and Yoko Ono on Fifth Avenue); rather, they're the personal defining life moments, such as winning a scholarship and going to college instead of working in the lumberyard.

❧ Sometimes the easiest way to start is simply by making lists. Here are some ideas for things you can list:

- beloved childhood toys, pets, comfort items (such as blankets and stuffed animals);
- favorite places as an adult as well as a child;
- family vacations;
- holidays spent with close friends and family members;
- clothes you wore as a child or to special occasions;
- major accomplishments in school, at home, on the job, or in the community;
- that special bicycle/car/truck/motorcycle you owned;
- awards you have received or those you have given to others;
- favorite books;
- favorite sports, games.

Jot down notes about anything that comes to mind from the items on the list. Writing down your memories often sets off even more memories and keeps you focused.

❧ Look in old photograph albums. Check out your family's scrapbooks. Watch old family movies and slides. There is a lot of useful detail in these sources. Seeing a picture of yourself at camp or on the first day of school can free up memories. Study the pictures closely for details such as

- dogs and cats sleeping on the floor;
- knickknacks on tables;
- chairs, tables, lamps;
- artwork hanging on the walls;
- shades and curtains;
- your hairstyle, eyeglasses, and jewelry;
- everyone's clothing;
- the expressions on everyone's faces, and so on.

❧ Look through the titles on your bookshelf because your favorite books and authors will stir up thoughts about specific times. Where did you read your Nancy Drew, Hardy Boys, or Harry Potter books? How did you feel about your college math professor? What thoughts does your family Bible bring back? Who was your favorite poet when you were a child?

❧ Thumb through your record collection or sheet music and list your favorite records, CDs, singers, and songs. Where were you when you first heard these songs? What were you doing? Who were you doing it with?

❧ What treasures did you save? I saved foreign money from my first trip out of the United States (it was to Canada), a token from my first ride on a New York City subway, and a ticket stub from the first Broadway show I saw. I even have a bottle of water from the first time I saw the ocean! Shaking the bottle brings back fond memories of my aunt (who *never* left the blanket) and my uncle (who *always* took me into the crashing surf). All my treasures have meaning only to me, of course.

Here are some other items you might use as inspiration:

e-mail, greeting cards, letters	dog tags
programs from grade school piano recitals	paper dolls
lists of school reunion class members	trading cards
report cards	yearbooks
collectibles, such as stamps, comics, coins	old magazines

Sort through your treasures to help you recall the story behind each object.

❧ Return to special places from your childhood. If you still live close to the town where you grew up, you might walk or drive past some of the places that were important in your life. For example, consider looking at your childhood apartment or house, playground, grade school, athletic fields, and so on. Revisiting the site or building can often help to bring back memories. For instance, when I revisited my elementary school playground recently, I was amazed at how small everything was. The swings seemed so far off the ground when I was a child.

❧ Study a time line of world events that took place when you were younger. Browse through some of these reference materials and see what pops out at you. I had a landmark birthday on July 20, 1969, when Neil Armstrong became the first person to walk on the moon. As a result, looking at a picture of the moon walk always brings back my birthday with crystal clarity. I remember exactly what I was doing and with whom. Find the world events that are linked to your life events. You can find world event time lines easily online or in books.

❧ What about inventions? I remember when we got our first clothes dryer, our first VCR, and our first touch-tone telephone. Recall what life was like before these inventions. What did people do before watching television was commonplace? (We played outside all the time.) Are there old-fashioned ways of doing things that you miss? You may think nobody's interested in hearing you talk about ice boxes, mangles, or carbon paper, but they are. I was born in the fifties, when Halloween was a great deal different from the way it is now. My kids can't believe the stories I tell them about trick-or-treating then.

Read Great Memoirs as Models

Throughout this book, I've provided you with models to give you ideas for your own creative writing. Models are a valuable way to structure and craft your writing. When it comes to memoirs, you might want to read those by some of the following writers. Warning: this list is highly idiosyncratic. I'm including just the names of my personal favorite memoirists.

Russell Baker	Tracy Kidder	George Orwell
Jill Ker Conway	Maxine Hong Kingston	David Sedaris
Annie Dillard	Primo Levi	Calvin Trillin
David Eggers	Mary McCarthy	Elie Wiesel
Ulysses S. Grant	Frank McCourt	Tobias Wolff

Study the following excerpt from the preface to Ulysses S. Grant's famous memoirs. What details make his memoir especially interesting? How does the chronological organization make it easy to follow his memories? How does his familiar, personal tone draw you into his writing?

Although frequently urged by friends to write my memoirs I had determined never to do so, nor to write anything for publication. At the age of nearly sixty-two I received an injury from a fall, which confined me closely to the house while it did not apparently affect my general health. This made study a pleasant pastime. Shortly after, the rascality of a business partner developed itself by the announcement of a failure. This was followed soon after by universal depression of all securities, which seemed to threaten the extinction of a good part of the income still retained, and for which I am indebted to the kindly act of friends. At this juncture the editor of the Century Magazine asked me to write a few articles for him. I consented for the money it gave me; for at that moment I was living upon borrowed money. The work I found congenial, and I determined to continue it. The event is an important one for me, for good or evil; I hope for the former.

In preparing these volumes for the public, I have entered upon the task with the sincere desire to avoid doing injustice to any one, whether on the National or Confederate side, other than the unavoidable injustice of not making mention often where special mention is due. There must be many errors of omission in this work, because the subject is too large to be treated of in two volumes in such way as to do justice to all the officers and men engaged. There were thousands of instances, during the rebellion, of individual, company, regimental and brigade deeds of heroism which deserve special mention and are not here alluded to. The troops engaged in them will have to look to the detailed reports of their individual commanders for the full history of those deeds. . . .

MOUNT MACGREGOR, NEW YORK, July 1, 1885.

The schools, at the time of which I write, were very indifferent. There were no free schools, and none in which the scholars were classified. They were all supported by subscription, and a single teacher—who was often a man or a woman incapable of teaching much, even if they imparted all they knew—would have thirty or forty scholars, male and female, from the infant learning the A B C's up to the young lady of eighteen and the boy of twenty, studying the highest branches taught—the three R's, "Reading, 'Riting, 'Rithmetic." I never saw an algebra, or other mathematical work higher than the arithmetic, in Georgetown, until after I was appointed to West Point. I then bought a work on algebra in Cincinnati; but having no teacher it was Greek to me.

My life in Georgetown was uneventful. From the age of five or six until seventeen, I attended the subscription schools of the village, except during the winters of 1836–7 and 1838–9. The former period was spent in Maysville, Kentucky, attending the school of Richardson and Rand; the latter in Ripley, Ohio, at a private school. I was not studious in habit, and probably did not make progress enough to compensate for the outlay for board and tuition. At all events both winters were spent in going over the same old arithmetic which I knew every word of before, and repeating: "A noun is the name of a thing," which I had also heard my Georgetown teachers repeat, until I had come to believe it—but I cast no reflections upon my old teacher, Richardson. He turned out bright scholars from his school, many of whom have filled conspicuous places in the service of their States. Two of my contemporaries there—who, I believe, never attended any other institution of learning—have held seats in Congress, and one, if not both, other high offices; these are Wadsworth and Brewster.

You can also visit MemoryArchive, a wiki Web site that allows anyone to record memories of notable people, places, events, or any other thing that others would consider of importance historically. Some people have written solemn entries on topics such as the

September 11 attacks, while others record humorous events. Consider skimming this Web site to get ideas for your own memoirs. The URL is http://www.memoryarchive.org. Later, you might want to add your memoir or a portion of it to this site.

> A *wiki* is a Web site that allows any user to create and edit its contents. Wiki, an abbreviation for WikiWiki Web, comes from a Hawaiian word that means "speed." On a wiki, one person can correct another person's posting. People can have discussions on a wiki as well. Different wikis have different rules, so read the FAQs (frequently asked questions) before you post anything on any wiki.

How to Draft Your Memoir

Now you're ready to start writing your memoir. First, organize your ideas. You can use a graphic organizer such as a storyboard. It's ideally suited to chronological order of events. It looks like this:

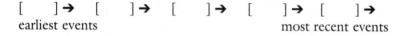

earliest events   most recent events

To make your memoir interesting and specific, include vivid details and sensory descriptions that appeal to the five senses. Describe sights, sounds, smells; use details that help your readers get a vivid mental picture of the person, place, or event you are describing.

Choose a Style

Recall that a writer's style is his or her distinctive way of writing. Style is made up of elements such as diction, sentence length and structure, figures of speech, and tone. Writers change their style for different kinds of writing and different audiences. When you write a memoir, write in your own style, in a manner that's natural for you. Concentrate on getting your ideas down on paper instead of fretting about grammar, spelling, and punctuation. You'll have an opportunity to revise and edit with subsequent drafts.

Decide on Dialogue

The issue of dialogue is controversial. On one hand, you know that dialogue makes your narrative writing fascinating. After all, who wants to read a story that has only pages and pages of description without any dialogue? These narratives can suffocate under the weight of detail. But on the other hand, no one can remember someone's exact words, especially years and years in the past. You want your memoir to be truthful, not fiction. Should you create conversations, personal thoughts, and other information you don't remember or never knew in the first place?

Here's an ethical way to resolve the issue: if you don't remember the dialogue or never heard it, interview people who do remember. See if you can interview the people who actually said the original words. To determine the accuracy of their memories, try to interview many eyewitnesses and participants and compare and contrast their accounts. See how they are the same and different.

Surround all direct quotes with quotation marks, like this: "I remember the time you had your tonsils out." Avoid altering someone's direct quotes, except for minor alterations for clarity. Enclose any information from already published material in quotation marks and be sure to give credit to the original authors.

Use Flashbacks and Flash-forwards

Sometimes you want to include scenes that aren't part of the strict chronology to explain an event, action, motivation, or reaction. You have two choices: flashbacks and flash-forwards. A *flashback* breaks into the story to show an earlier part of the action. A *flash-forward* shows a later part of the action.

Overcome Writer's Block

Having trouble drafting? Try writing just one page a day—that's right, just one. Setting such an easy deadline takes off the pressure. Best of all, if you write just one page a day for a year, you'll have 365 pages at the end of the year. Before you know it, you'll have an entire memoir written.

How to Publish Your Memoir

Some people choose to share their memoir; others decide to keep it private. Of course, the decision is purely personal. However, if you do decide to publish your memoir, there are many easy ways to do so. Consider these ideas:

❧ Publish online, on your blog or Web page. I have posted chapters of my memoir on my blog and my Web page, but if you don't want to set up a blog or a Web page, or you want a much wider audience than your blog is likely to attract, you can add your memoir to MemoryArchive, the wiki Web site that you read about earlier in this chapter.

❧ Bring your electronic file or a hard copy to a copy center and have copies printed and bound. Some copy centers and printers can accept e-mailed files, so you won't even need to leave your house. Then you can distribute the copies as you please. (This method of publication is surprisingly affordable.)

❧ Package your memoir as a book by using a self-publishing company. Traditionally called vanity presses, these companies can produce hardcover or softcover copies at a reasonable cost. You can locate the names of these companies online or in the telephone book.

❧ If you have included photographs and even videos, you may wish to burn a CD. You can then distribute your memoir as a CD or have it printed as a hard copy.

No matter which method of publication you choose, consider donating a copy of your memoir to your local historical society or library.

You Must Remember This
Speaking of her memoir, mystery writer Agatha Christie once wrote: "Autobiography is too grand a term. It suggests a purposeful study of one's whole life. It implies names, dates, and places in a tidy chronological order. What I want is to plunge my hand into a lucky dip and come up with a handful of assorted memories."

Plunge your hand into a "lucky dip" and write *your* memoirs. Sit right down and start writing today. You'll really be glad you did.

CHAPTER 9
Writing Creative Narratives

—∞∞∞—

A Crow, half-dead with thirst, came upon a Pitcher which had once been full of water; but when the Crow put its beak into the mouth of the Pitcher he found that only very little water was left in it, and that he could not reach far enough down to get at it. He tried, and he tried, but at last had to give up in despair. Then a thought came to him, and he took a pebble and dropped it into the Pitcher. Then he took another pebble and dropped it into the Pitcher. Then he took another pebble and dropped that into the Pitcher . . . and another . . . and another . . . and another. At long last, the Crow saw the water mount up near him, and after casting in a few more pebbles he was able to quench his thirst and save his life.

—Aesop Fable, "The Crow and the Pitcher"

The moral of this story is that little by little does the trick. The same moral applies to creative writing: write one page, another page, one more page . . . and before you know it, you'll have completed an entire project.

Everyone loves a good story because stories entertain us, instruct us, and unite us. For a creative writer, few genres are as much fun to write as a narrative. But narratives can seem a bit daunting because there's so much to remember: plot, characters, setting, dialogue, point of view, theme, and even more. Relax! All you have to do is write one page at a time, and soon you'll have a completed narrative.

Narrative Forms

They say variety is the spice of life, and nowhere is this truer than in narrative forms. We have short narrative forms and long narrative forms, old narrative forms and new narrative forms. As a result, you can choose the narrative form that best suits your interests and unlocks your imagination. Here are some of the most common narrative forms:

Shorter forms	**Longer forms**
comics	epics
fables	graphic novels
flash fiction	novels
folk tales and fairy tales	romans à clef
short stories	

Now for some definitions:

Type of Narrative	Definition
Flash fiction	very short stories, usually 1,000–2,000 words
Fable	a short, easy-to-read story that teaches a lesson about people. Fables often feature animals that talk and act like people.
Folk tales	have been handed down from generation to generation. Fables, fairy tales, legends, tall tales, and myths are different types of folktales. Many folktales contain unusual characters and a moral (a lesson).
Fairy tale	a type of folk tale
Short story	narrative prose fiction shorter than a novel that focuses on a single character and a single event. Most short stories can be read in one sitting and convey a single overall impression. They are usually 2,000–7,500 words.
Comics	narratives that tell the story through words and pictures. The pictures are presented in a series of panels.

Novel	a long work of fiction, usually 60,000 words or more. The elements of a novel—plot, characterizations, setting, and theme—are developed in detail. Novels usually have one main plot and several less important subplots.
Roman à clef	a novel that describes thinly disguised real-life events
Epics	long fictional narratives of 200,000 words or more. Epics usually recount a hero's great adventures and achievements. They are often written in a formal, elevated style. Alone of all the narrative forms listed here, epics can be written in poetry as well as prose (nonpoetry).
Graphic novels	long comic books that tell the story through drawings as well as words

These types of narratives can be subdivided into specific types of novels and short stories, such as romance novels, adventure novels, horror stories and horror novels, and so on. No matter which narrative form you choose to write, they all share the same elements. As a result, when you learn one form, you can adapt what you learned to writing other forms as well.

> *Science fiction* is fantasy writing that tells about make-believe events that include science or technology. Often science fiction is set in the future, on distant planets, or among alien races.

Short Story Warm-Up
In a few minutes, I'll teach you the elements in a narrative. First, enough reading—it's time to warm-up those writing muscles! Look at the following photograph for a few minutes and then write a brief story based on what you see. What elements in the picture triggered your imagination?

Evert F. Baumgardner, c. 1958. National Archives and Records Administration.

> How long should your stories be? Make each story just long enough to tell what you need it to tell.

As promised, here are the elements that make up every narrative. I've arranged them in the order that most writers approach them as they plan a story:

Point of View
Point of view is the position from which a story is told. Here are the three points of view from which you can choose:

❧ *First person:* The narrator is one of the characters in the story. The narrator explains the events through his or her own eyes, using the pronouns *I* and *me*. You may wish to use the first-person point of view to give your stories an immediacy, intimacy, and drama. The first-person point of view is also a good choice when you

want to slant the events, since the narrator doesn't have
to tell the truth.

✤ *Third person omniscient:* The narrator is not a character
in the story. Instead, the narrator looks through the eyes
of all the characters. As a result, the narrator is all knowing. The narrator uses the pronouns *he, she,* and *they.*

✤ *Third person limited:* The narrator tells the story
through the eyes of only one character, using the pronouns *he, she,* and *they.*

Remember: the *narrator* is the person who tells a story. The narrator may also be a character in the work.

Here's the same incident told from two different points of view.
How does the change in point of view alter your perception of the
main character?

Point of View 1: First Person
*Uplifting an axe, and forgetting, in my wrath, the childish
dread which had hitherto stayed my hand, I aimed a blow at the
animal which, of course, would have proved instantly fatal had
it descended as I wished. But this blow was arrested by the hand
of my wife. Goaded, by the interference, into a rage more than
demoniacal, I withdrew my arm from her grasp and buried the
axe in her brain. She fell dead upon the spot, without a groan.*
—Edgar Allan Poe, "The Black Cat"

Point of View 2: Third Person Omniscient
*Uplifting an axe, and forgetting, in his wrath, the childish
dread which had hitherto stayed his hand, Leo aimed a blow at
the animal which, of course, would have proved instantly fatal
had it descended as he wished. But this blow was arrested by the
hand of his wife, Muriel. Goaded, by the interference, into a rage
that seemed demoniacal, Leo withdrew his arm from her grasp
and buried the axe in her brain. She fell dead upon the spot,
without a groan. It served Muriel right because she had been*

preparing to poison Leo, but Leo was going to have an unfairly
hard time proving that his act was justified.

In the first excerpt, we see the events through the narrator's eyes
only. We don't know if the narrator is telling the truth, since we
have only his account of the incident. In the second excerpt, we're
seeing the same action from an outside point of view. This narrator is all knowing, as shown by the last sentence. The first excerpt
has the advantage of immediacy and drama; the second, of com-
pleteness.

Select the point of view carefully because it affects how your
readers respond to your characters. Readers are influenced not
only by how much the narrator seems to know but also by the
narrator's trustworthiness.

Plot

The *plot* is the arrangement of events in a work of literature. Plots
have a beginning, middle, and end. The writer arranges the events
of the plot to keep the reader's interest and convey the theme.

❧ The *climax* of a plot is the highest point in the action.
During the climax, the conflict is resolved and the end
of the story becomes clear. The climax is also called the
turning point.

❧ The *resolution* (or *denouement)* occurs near the end when
the writer has woven all the plot elements together.

Here's how a traditional short story plot looks in diagram
form:

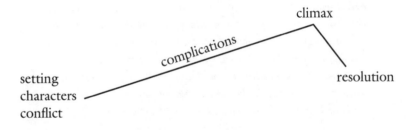

Writers vary the structure of their plots depending on the story. For example, in a mystery story, the writer will withhold plot exposition until later to build suspense and tension. As you plan the plot of each story, ask yourself, "How can I arrange the story elements to tell the story in the best possible way?" You want the story clear but also suspenseful. You want to control the reader's emotional responses.

Theme

Theme is the narrative's main idea, a general statement about life. The writer can state the theme directly in the narrative, as is the case with most fables. In other narratives, readers will have to infer the theme from details about plot, characters, and setting.

How can you create the theme in your short stories? While plot, setting, and characters combine to make the theme apparent, you can also use these three techniques:

❧ repeat key patterns and symbols
❧ make reference to a well-known place, event, person, work of art, or other work of literature
❧ insert key details that suggest larger meanings

Fables are ideal models to use as you create your themes because the narrative is concise and the theme is clear. What do you think is the theme of this fable?

> *A Fox once saw a Crow fly off with a piece of cheese in its beak and settle on a branch of a tree. "That's for me, as I am a Fox," said Master Reynard, and he walked up to the foot of the tree. "Good-day, Mistress Crow," he cried. "How well you are looking to-day: how glossy your feathers; how bright your eye. I feel sure your voice must surpass that of other birds, just as your figure does; let me hear but one song from you that I may greet you as the Queen of Birds." The Crow lifted up her head and began to caw her best, but the moment she opened her mouth the piece of cheese fell to the ground, only to be snapped up by Master Fox. "That will do," said he. "That was all I wanted." And he ran away.*

Use story clues to infer the theme. First, you know that certain animals are known for specific character traits: ants and beavers are thought to be hardworking, rats and snakes are considered sneaky, and foxes are thought to be wily. Sure enough, the author works with these conventions. We see this as the fox cleverly flatters the crow. The fox says: "How glossy your feathers; how bright your eye. I feel sure your voice must surpass that of other birds, just as your figure does; let me hear but one song from you that I may greet you as the Queen of Birds." Third, the fox does succeed in getting the piece of cheese. Putting these clues together, you can figure out the theme: do not trust flatterers. Plant thematic clues like this as you construct your narratives.

Here are some traditional themes that you might wish to use as you get started. Remember, the theme doesn't have to be new and fresh, but the way you develop it does.

- ❧ Do unto others as you would have them do unto you.
- ❧ United we stand, divided we fall.
- ❧ You can't please everyone.
- ❧ Misery loves company.
- ❧ Look before you leap.
- ❧ Time is money.
- ❧ Leave well enough alone.
- ❧ Slow and steady wins the race.
- ❧ Waste not, want not.
- ❧ Someone may smile but still be a villain.

Conflict

Conflict is a struggle or fight in a narrative. Conflict makes a story interesting because readers want to find out the outcome. There are two kinds of conflict: external and internal. In an *external conflict,* characters struggle against a force outside themselves. In an *internal conflict,* characters battle a force within themselves. Stories often contain both external and internal conflicts.

The conflict must contain *suspense,* the feeling of tension or anticipation an author creates in a work. Authors create suspense by unexpected plot twists to keep readers interested in the story and make them want to read on to find out what will happen.

Conflict doesn't necessarily mean violence. In your narratives, your main character will have a specific need, goal, or purpose that he or she wants to attain, but something is standing in the way. The main character struggles to overcome the opposition. He or she may win or lose. It's the struggle that engages your readers.

Setting

The *setting* of a story is the time and place where the events take place. Sometimes you'll state the setting outright: "It was a beautiful sunny day in Meadville." Other times, however, you'll have readers infer the setting from details in the story. You'll plant clues in the characters' speech, clothing, or means of transportation. To quote from Edgar Allan Poe, it depends on what "single effect" you want to create in your story.

> A *symbol* is a person, place, or object that represents an abstract idea. For example, a dove often symbolizes peace, and a rose often symbolizes love. Without cultural agreement, many of the symbols we commonly accept would be meaningless.

Symbolic Settings

A story's setting is always important, but some settings are more important than others, functioning as symbols. This is true of the short stories in Sherwood Anderson's famous novel *Winesburg, Ohio,* where the anonymous small Midwestern town symbolizes the characters' emotional isolation. Here's an excerpt from a story in the collection called "Hands." The main character, Wing Biddlebaum, has been made into what Anderson calls a "grotesque" because of the isolation caused by the setting. As you read the following excerpt, see how the setting symbolizes Wing himself, "seeded for clover [something valuable] but that had produced only a dense crop of yellow mustard weeds [something disappointing and valueless]."

Upon the half decayed veranda of a small frame house that stood near the edge of a ravine near the town of Winesburg, Ohio, a fat little old man walked nervously up and down. Across a long field that had been seeded for clover but that had produced only a dense crop of yellow mustard weeds, he could see the public high-

*way along which went a wagon filled with berry pickers return-
ing from the fields. The berry pickers, youths and maidens,
laughed and shouted boisterously. A boy clad in a blue shirt
leaped from the wagon and attempted to drag after him one of
the maidens, who screamed and protested shrilly. The feet of the
boy in the road kicked up a cloud of dust that floated across the
face of the departing sun. Over the long field came a thin girlish
voice. "Oh, you Wing Biddlebaum, comb your hair, it's falling
into your eyes," commanded the voice to the man, who was bald
and whose nervous little hands fiddled about the bare white fore-
head as though arranging a mass of tangled locks.*

Techniques for Creating Setting

Setting is created by language. How many—or how few—details
you include is completely your decision. You may want to describe
the setting in great detail or leave much of it up to the reader's
imagination. As I've emphasized, one of the best ways to learn a
writing technique is by studying models. Use the Sherwood
Anderson model (as well as other novels and stories) as you craft
the settings for your own narratives.

Character and Characterization

A *character* is a person or an animal in a story. *Main characters*
have important roles in the narrative; *minor characters* have smaller parts. A minor character serves as a contrast to the main character or to advance the plot. The main character is also called the
protagonist. The *protagonist* is at the center of the conflict and the
focus of our attention. An *antagonist* is the force or person in conflict with the main character in a narrative. An antagonist can be
another character, a force of nature, society, or something within
the character.

Don't be fooled: major characters don't have to be dynamic.
Also, you might create a major character who doesn't even appear
in the story. The story might revolve around the reactions of the
other characters to this one individual.

You create unforgettable characters through *characterization,*
the different ways that you tell your readers about characters.
Sometimes you tell about characters directly. Other times, you
might decide to let readers reach their own decisions by showing

the comments, thoughts, and actions of the other characters. Here are some elements of characterization:

actions	dialogue and dialect
clothing	physical traits

Your reader has to be able to visualize your characters. This doesn't mean that your characters have to be based on real people, or that readers have to like your characters. But if your readers aren't interested in your characters, they won't want to read your story.

The more you know about your characters, the easier it will be for you to make your readers feel as if they know them too. You can create a character trait web to help you flesh out your characters. Feel free to modify the number of traits as necessary to fit the character and the story. Examples can come directly from details you will include in the story or be based on inferences that readers will make.

Start by writing the character's name in the middle of the web. Then add details and examples.

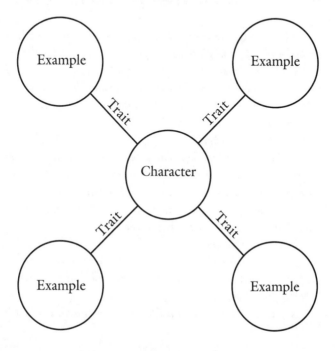

Stuck for character traits? Here are some traits to get you started: *audacious, affectionate, bighearted, bold, candid, deceitful, depressed, devoted, introverted, malicious, modest, nationalistic, ruthless, self-centered, sluggish.*

Dialogue and Dialect

Dialogue is the conversation in fiction or drama. It is the exact words a character says. In a story or novel, quotation marks are used to point out the dialogue.

Dialect is the way people speak in a certain region or area. In a dialect, certain words are spelled and pronounced differently. You might wish to use dialects to describe the characters and setting more fully. Here's an example from Mark Twain's novel *The Adventures of Huckleberry Finn*. Huck is talking to his father, Pap, a cruel drunk. As you read, notice how Twain spells certain words to capture the way that people really spoke at that time and in that place:

> *He set there a-mumbling and a-growling a minute, and then he says:*
>
> *"AIN'T you a sweet-scented dandy, though? A bed; and bed-clothes; and a look'n'-glass; and a piece of carpet on the floor—and your own father got to sleep with the hogs in the tanyard. I never see such a son. I bet I'll take some o' these frills out o' you before I'm done with you. Why, there ain't no end to your airs—they say you're rich. Hey?—how's that?"*
>
> *"They lie—that's how."*
>
> *"Looky here—mind how you talk to me; I'm a-standing about all I can stand now—so don't gimme no sass. I've been in town two days, and I hain't heard nothing but about you bein' rich. I heard about it away down the river, too. That's why I come. You git me that money to-morrow—I want it."*
>
> *"I hain't got no money."*
>
> *"It's a lie. Judge Thatcher's got it. You git it. I want it."*
>
> *"I hain't got no money, I tell you. You ask Judge Thatcher; he'll tell you the same."*
>
> *"All right. I'll ask him; and I'll make him pungle, too, or I'll*

know the reason why. Say, how much you got in your pocket? I want it."

"I hain't got only a dollar, and I want that to—"

"It don't make no difference what you want it for—you just shell it out."

You'll want to use a lot of dialogue in your stories to create characterization and advance the plot. That's because dialogue helps you reveal your characters' traits rather than mere descriptions. The famous advice is "Show, don't tell" in a narrative.

Express Your Unique Writing Style

Breathe life into the characters, conflict, and setting by using your personal, unique writing style. You'll want to include sensory details to make your stories fresh and unforgettable. Describe how things taste, smell, look, feel, and sound. Use concrete details that help readers form vivid mental images. Here's an example:

Weak Style:

Nick enjoyed walking through country graveyards on fall afternoons. He enjoyed looking at the marble tablets with their ornate, old-fashioned inscriptions. They made him remember how sad he felt when his grandfather died last year.

Strong Style:

I remember my grandfather's funeral—the hurried cross of sand the minister drew on the coffin lid; the whine of the lowering straps; the lengthening, cleanly cut sides of soil; the lack of air forever in the close, dark coffin.

Let's isolate the details in the second passage:

Sense	Detail
sight	"the lengthening, cleanly cut sides of soil"
sound	"the whine of the lowering straps"
smell	"the lengthening, cleanly cut sides of soil"
feel	"cross of sand the minister drew on the coffin lid . . . the lack of air forever in the close, dark coffin."

Add a Title

Sometimes a story is sparked by a title; other times, you'll add the title last, as you would icing on a delicious cake. Whether you start with the title or finish with it, the following suggestions will help you craft memorable titles:

- ❧ *Keep it brief.* Some writers argue that a title should be no more than six words long. I say: make your title as long or as short as you need.

- ❧ *Make it enticing.* Create titles that make your readers want to read your story. You might quote a snatch of a song lyric, for example, or create a pun (a play on words).

- ❧ *Explore different forms.* Your story's title can be a label, statement, question, command, or a combination of different forms (such as a statement that functions as a label).

You Must Remember This

A narrative is a story. You can write many different kinds of narratives, including fables, fairy tales, short stories, novels, romans à clef, and graphic novels (if you can also draw!). Regardless of the form your narrative takes, all narratives contain the following elements: point of view (the vantage point from which you chose to tell the story), plot (the events in the narrative), and theme (your message about life). Narratives also have conflict (a struggle that creates reader interest through suspense), setting (when and where the narrative takes place), and characters (the people). Dialogue is an important part of your style because it helps make your narratives interesting.

There's a lot of material in this chapter so it might seem a bit overwhelming. Remember: you don't have to develop these elements in the order in which I have presented them. You might discover the theme after you have completed your first draft, for example, rather than consciously planning it in the beginning. Or you might change all the characters or even the setting as you revise.

It takes most creative writers a long time to learn our craft. So keep at it. Don't give up.

$\mathscr{C}$HAPTER 10
Becoming Known as a Writer

I clearly remember the feeling I had soon after I was married when someone first referred to me as "Mrs. Rozakis"—I looked behind myself to see where my mother-in-law was standing. You see, it had not yet dawned on me that *I* was now a Mrs. Rozakis; I still thought of myself by my maiden name. It took me a surprisingly long time to identify myself as Mrs. Rozakis. I knew the day had finally come when I looked for myself in my high school yearbook, but my picture wasn't there. "How can this be?" I thought. "I was on the yearbook staff!" You've probably guessed that I was looking under Rozakis rather than my maiden name.

I had the same feeling the first time someone referred to me as a "writer." I was a teacher, a wife, and a mother—but not a writer. "They're dressing me in borrowed robes," I thought, yet I was indeed a writer. I wrote a lot and had even published several books and articles. It took a long time before I was comfortable identifying myself as a writer. In this chapter, I'm going to help you make the transition from your current career role to writer.

Identity Crisis
We all adopt a variety of different identities as we pass through the journey of life. How many of these roles have you fulfilled?

child	employee
teenager	manager
young married	widow or widower
aunt or uncle	retiree
mother or father	grandparent

Any change in identity is challenging because it comes with a new set of expectations. Thinking of yourself as a grandparent is very different from thinking of yourself as a parent, for example. (I'm not sure how I'll take it!) Some roles are more difficult to assume than others, however, because they deviate from what others expect of us.

It's not unusual for people to mature, create new families, and assume careers; after all, aren't most of our friends and neighbors identified one way or the other by their age, family position, or job? However, it *is* unusual for someone to become a writer. I knew only one professional writer during all the years I was growing up. Even though this successful man made his living as a writer, we lumped him in with all the other men who "went to work." I usually just thought of him as "my friend Peggy's father," even though he had a very distinguished career as a writer. The concept that he was a real *writer* was simply too momentous to accept.

If you write, you are a writer. I know, that's easy to say but much more difficult to believe. One way to help think of yourself as a writer is to become involved with a community of writers. You can do this easily by entering writing contests and by applying for writing grants. After a few prizes and checks, it will be easier for you—and everyone around you—to realize that you are indeed a "real" writer.

> Today you can hobnob with writers by e-mail. You can even form your own virtual writer's group. More on this later.

Appearance Versus Reality

For the past several years I have been privileged to moderate a wonderful writers' group. We meet at a local bookstore once a month for an hour and a half. The group has been terrifically successful in many ways.

❧ Everyone is producing some superb writing. Several people are working on novels, a few on short stories, and many on essays. One man who brings us special pride has written more than fifteen sensitive and evocative short stories while teaching full time. Another great writer has completed half a wonderful young adult novel while working full time. At least four people are writing memoirs, and nearly everyone is keeping a journal.

ᴥ My writers have learned to give—and accept—constructive criticism. This has resulted in some brilliant editing.

ᴥ And the icing on the cake? Many of my writers have been published! I know their success is the result of their talent and hard work, and that's why it cuts like a knife when they fall prey to a writing scam.

Last month, for example, one of our most talented and dedicated poets came in with notices about three "awards" he had received. Two were very impressive indeed: Tom had been awarded "first place" in two nationwide poetry contests.

Now, Tom is a fine poet, but it's virtually impossible for a newcomer to win two nationwide writing contests right out of the gate. I was immediately suspicious. Here are his prizes, so you can judge for yourself.

Prize Number One: Nationwide Publication
Tom's poem would be published in a beautiful book of poems. The book was big and impressive, and from the photograph of the previous edition, it looked as if it might even be leatherbound and gold tooled. All he had to do to collect his award was purchase the book. It was a real steal, too, at only a hundred dollars.

Prize Number Two: Publication and a National Ceremony
The second award was a bit pricier. To pick up this one, Tom had to travel to the "Annual Poet's Convention" in Washington, D.C. The airfare, room, and board were all on him. In addition, he had to pay five hundred dollars for admission. So this "award" would probably set him back two thousand dollars.

Prize Number Three: Publication and a Local Reading
The third award looked tacky in comparison to the first two, like Cinderella before her transformation. One of Tom's shorter poems had been selected for publication in a local anthology of Long Island poetry. The book was a slim, unimpressive paperback printed in only two colors. The publisher had sent him five copies, free of charge. Tom had also been invited to a reception for the winners. He could read his poem to the audience and have cake and coffee, provided by the local poet's organization.

Which award was the best? Prize number three was the only real prize. The first two awards were scams. Even though the local chapbook wasn't very impressive looking, this was actually quite a significant award because it conferred genuine recognition. In addition, it could lead to wider notice.

How can you tell that a writing prize is genuine? Here are some of the benchmarks:

❧ If it sounds too good to be true, it is. A novice writer is unlikely to win a major award. In nearly all cases, writers have to work their way up the ladder, as in most worthwhile endeavors. They begin by winning local awards, then regional, and finally national. Competition is fierce, especially for first prizes in big-money national awards. While a newcomer *can* win a major writing prize, it is a rare occurrence.

❧ You should never have to pay to receive your award. Nearly all writing competitions carry a small entrance fee, often around fifteen to twenty-five dollars. This fee covers the cost of funding the prize and enriching the organization's coffers. However, an *entrance* fee is very different from a *prize* fee.

❧ Be leery of contest publications that look very expensive. It's unusual today for publishers to be issuing rich leatherbound and gold-tooled books for any market, never mind prizewinners. Check the shelves of your local book store: you'll see plain paper bindings. Further, many books come out originally in paperback, bypassing the clothbound stage. If you see prizewinning writing in a gorgeous book, ask yourself who is paying the extra publishing cost. Chances are very good that it's the "prizewinner."

❧ Check the source of the award. The vast majority of legitimate writing contests are sponsored by universities, colleges, the government, and writers' organizations. This is logical for many reasons. First, schools want to identify fine writers to hire as teachers. Second, the government wants to recognize fine writers as cultural treasures. Finally, writers' organizations exist to help writers. Some rich individuals fund writing prizes, too, but they usually work through universities, writers' groups, and arts foundations, so they're easy to identify. Why would a private organization want to give a writer a prize? The answer: to get money—your money. Nowadays it's easy to check the legitimacy of a writing contest on the Web, since there are scam-alert pages that list fraudulent awards.

❧ Check the names of other winners. Ask for the names and e-mail addresses of past winners. Contact some of these people and check out their experiences with the organization. Was the contest on the level? Were they asked for money? How was their writing eventually used? It might never have been published, or it was distributed in disappointingly limited quantities.

Before you're carried away with the joy of "winning," make sure that you have won a real award. Since forewarned is forearmed, let's turn to the legitimate writing contests that you might wish to enter. Entering and winning writing contests is a great way to help you recognize your talent as a writer. From there it's just a brief step to identifying yourself as a *writer*.

If you do enter a contest with an entry fee (on- or off-line), pay by credit card. In the unlikely event you're cheated, you have your credit card company on your side to help you resolve the issue.

Why Enter a Writing Contest?

Using the keywords *writing contests*, I found 2,250,000 sites, which proves there's no shortage of writing contests. Assuming that half these entries may not be legitimate contests, which is a safe assumption, you can still conclude that there are a lot of writing contests. This means that there's a writing contest for everyone's talent and more than enough contests to go around. Therefore, your dilemma shouldn't be whether or not to enter a writing contest, but which ones to enter. Here are some specific reasons to enter writing contests:

❧ Writing contests give you concrete goals. It is a lot of work entering a writing contest, so why bother? First of all, entering a writing contest gives you a clear goal because you must produce a specific document within a specific time. For example, one contest gives you the choice of submitting a poem (thirty lines or less), a short story (fewer than a thousand words), or an essay (fewer than a thousand words). You have a one-month deadline.

❧ Writing contests help you remember your readers. Entering a writing contest also teaches you to write for a specific audience. Perhaps up to now you have been writing for yourself. It's a good idea to branch out and write for others as well.

❧ Writing contests reinforce the importance of meeting deadlines. Further, entering contests helps you learn to set and meet deadlines just like professional writers. Time management is a vitally important skill to develop as a writer, and entering contests can help you master this skill.

⤙ Writing contests teach you to be precise. Creative writers are, well, creative! As a result, we're not usually noted for our ability to follow directions. This is not necessarily a negative trait when it comes to unleashing our imagination. But being free and easy can be detrimental when it comes to meeting an editor's needs. Entering writing contests teaches us how to follow directions. Another contest that I found online, for example, requires that the entry be submitted electronically, in the body of an e-mail, not as an attachment. This contest specifies that each entry should include the following information at the bottom of the e-mail: name, pen name (if any), e-mail address, and mailing address. Participants can send in as many works as they like. Completing these requirements is easy but does require close attention to detail.

⤙ Writing contests can give you useful feedback. In addition, rejections have their uses. After you lick your wounds, you realize that rejections can offer useful criticism and advice. Weighing what the judges say can help you find a balance between what you believe about your work and what others have to say. Over the years, you'll start to develop a distance from your writing so you'll be more able to handle negative suggestions and not be crushed by rejection.

⤙ Writing contests help refresh your imagination as you switch gears. Last but certainly not least, writing contests can give you a much needed breather from routine but still help you keep writing. This can enrich your other writing and help you get unstuck if you're having difficulty working out a passage. For instance, say you're stuck on a page of your memoir. You may want to enter a writing contest to give yourself a chance to step back and regroup while still writing. Many writers switch genres for a break.

Rumor has it that Oliver Stone received over a thousand formal rejection letters from Hollywood producers before he made any headway. Talk about perseverance!

Ways to Find Out About Contests

The Internet is a great source for writing-contest information, as I discussed earlier in the chapter. Use "writing contests" as your keywords. If you're not comfortable using a computer, most large public libraries carry lists of funding sources for writers. Ask at the reference desk.

How to Enter a Writing Contest

It's surprisingly easy to enter most writing contests, but because I help judge a prestigious university poetry contest, I've seen *all* the ways that writers can go wrong. So that this doesn't happen to you, let me share my experience as an entrant, a judge, and a winner. The following guidelines can help ensure that your entries go to the top of the stack.

- ❧ Actually enter the contest. This sounds obvious, but you can't win it if you're not in it. Talking about it, thinking about it, dreaming about it—none of these will actually do any good unless you write and submit the entry. Many contest winners talk about how they almost didn't enter; don't let this happen to you.

- ❧ Read the contest directions carefully. My husband jokes that I never read to the bottom of a document. Unfortunately, he's right. Don't make my mistake, especially when it comes to writing contests. The fine print *always* matters.

- ❧ Follow the contest guidelines *exactly*. First and foremost, make sure you qualify for the specific contest you want to enter. Read the guidelines carefully to make sure you don't enter a contest for which you're not qualified. Consider the writer's age because some contests are open only to writers who are specific ages (under twenty-one, over fifty, and so on). Also consider the issue of previous publication. Sometimes you must be a published author to qualify for the contest; other times, in contrast, you must be unpublished. Sometimes it doesn't matter whether or not you've published before. Geographic location can also be a factor in some contests. Where you live can occasionally make you eligible or ineligible for certain contests. Further, the genre of writing can be a big consideration. Most contests solicit specific genres and subgenres, such as essays or short stories. Then make sure you follow the entrance rules to the letter. For instance, if the contest says to "handwrite on a 3-x-5 index card," then that is what you will do. If the guidelines say, "Write your name on the cover sheet. Do not put your name on the story," write your name on the cover sheet and do not put your name on the story. Also, be very sure to stay within the word count. Check, double-check, and triple-check the guidelines and your compliance with them. If you follow the guidelines and write to your best ability, then winning can become a reality.

❧ Do your research. First, research the contest itself. Be sure to get the very latest writing-contest information available. Some groups lose their funding; some publications fold. Don't waste your time unless you know the contest information is timely and accurate. Then read some of the previous winning entries to get insight into the types of writing that impressed previous judges. You're never going to copy these past works; rather, you're going to make sure that your entry fits the contest parameters. If it doesn't, you're wasting your time with this particular contest and should try some others.

❧ Play the odds. The more contests you enter, the greater your chances of winning. Now, I am *not* telling you to enter every contest you hear about willy-nilly. However, I *am* suggesting that you try to enter several contests to maximize your chances of striking gold. To this end, build up a growing portfolio of your best writing. Polish and refine these pieces so you can submit the best and most appropriate ones. This approach will not only maximize your chances of winning contests but also (and more importantly) develop your craft as a writer.

❧ Be professional in your presentation. Check and double-check your spelling and punctuation. Print any hard copies on a high-quality printer unless you're required to handwrite it. As a judge, I can attest that few things are as annoying as not being able to read the entry because of a poor-quality copy.

> If you're applying for an award sponsored by a print or online magazine, read several issues of the magazine to familiarize yourself with its style.

Going for Grants

Another way to support your writing is to get funding from foundations and agencies. There's a surprising amount of money available. Private groups, service organizations, and state agencies are three of the sources to consider first.

Foundations invest in deserving people (that's *you*) and expect a return. I received my first grant in 1986, an Empire State Challenger Fellowship. It was renewed the following year. That was quickly followed by a whole series of grants. Here are some of the most noteworthy ones:

Joint Labor/Management Committee Individual
    Development Award $1,000

Joint Labor/Management Committee Individual
    Development Award $500

Porter Fellowship (American Federation of Teachers)
    $1,000

Farmingdale College Foundation Faculty Merit Award
    $3,000

As you can see, the same agency has awarded me a grant more than once. That's common; once you've proven your worth, you can often get additional funding from the same source.

How can you win a grant? Get involved in your local or state arts council through programs and panels. Network to find other sources of funding. Here are some additional ideas:

✎ Check your library for workshops on grant writing.

✎ Attend free community lectures at local universities, colleges, and schools. Ask the sponsors how they came to hire and fund the speaker.

✎ Give readings of your work at schools, hospitals, retirement homes, community functions. Service groups such as the American Association of University Women, the Women's Club, and Rotary are always looking for free speakers to entertain at their meetings.

✎ Write a history of your town, community, or region.

✎ Write a biography about a famous person in the area or in the foundation.

You Must Remember This

There's a lot of money available to writers. Enter writing contests and apply for grants to get funding. Entering contests can not only help you win support but also help you hone your craft and meet other writers. Many prizes carry publication as well as money. These successes will help you—as well as others—see yourself as a creative writer.

$\mathscr{C}$HAPTER 11
Sharing Your Work

You can write for your own pleasure, for the sheer joy of writing, and I'll say, "Enjoy yourself!" However, the day may come when you decide it's time to share your words with someone else. "Publishing" can be as formal as a three-book deal with a major publishing company or as informal as reading your essay aloud in writers' groups. Or it can be both and many options in between.

That's another great advantage of creative writing; you *can* have it your way. In this chapter, we'll explore some of the options for sharing your creative writing so that you can decide which ones are right for you now and in the future.

Joining a Writers' Group

I'm a big fan of writers' groups. How can you tell? I belong to two different writers' groups and moderate another one! Being part of a writers' group is the easiest way to share your work. Let me tell you all about my groups so you can decide if this method of publication and networking suits your interests and lifestyle.

My New York City Writers' Group

We formed this group about twenty years ago when a handful of my writer friends and I decided to band together for support and survival. We chose to meet in New York City because it's the most central location, since we hail from New Jersey, Long Island, Connecticut, and every borough of New York. We meet in casual Manhattan restaurants, usually Chinese places or buffets, so that everyone can join in without regard to budget constraints.

At our frequent meetings, we discuss one another's current writing projects, swap news about the companies we deal with, and share our experiences as writers. At one point, we had more than thirty writers coming to meetings, but that proved too cumbersome, so now we're a core group of about twelve writers.

I have found this writers' group to be a tremendous help personally and professionally. We alert one another to jobs and pay rates. We celebrate one another's triumphs and support one another during tragedies. These friends and colleagues are able to support my writing career because they understand it so well. They're also a great group of people whom I've come to respect deeply as friends as well as writers.

My Long Island Writers' Group

I also moderate a fairly large writers' group, varying from twenty to twenty-five members. We meet formally in a local bookstore once a month for an hour and a half. Our members include nurses, homemakers, teachers, laborers, lawyers, and many retirees.

Although none of the members has published through conventional channels, this group tends to be more formal than my other group. Here we come equipped with sufficient copies of our work to share with each attendee. We take turns presenting our work for discussion, constructive criticism, and praise. I rarely present my work, however, because I'm too busy moderating the discussion. However, when I am having difficulty working out a specific section of an essay or book, I do bring copies to share with the group. I find that my fellow writers are a fine sounding board, offering insightful comments and suggestions for improvements.

My Online Group

I've never met a single member of my third writers' group, because we're scattered all across the globe. One member lives in India part of the year; another has a winter house in Florida. Several others live in California, and a few make their home in Oregon and Washington State. I don't even know where several others live. Nonetheless, we're in contact almost daily. How is this possible? Thank the Internet.

As with my New York City group, in my virtual writers' group we share industry news about publishing companies going in and out of business, editors moving on to new jobs, and payment rates fluctuating. We also ask for feedback about one another's work and offer support when the muse has fled. Since this group is so varied, I get wildly different viewpoints, which I find enormously helpful.

Your group might be small or large, formal or informal. It might meet in person or communicate solely through the Internet. You might even belong to more than one writers' group, as I do. The choice is yours.

Organizing a Writers' Group

Now that I've got you eager to join a writers' group, how can you get started? First, see if a group already exists in your community. Local writers often organize groups through the public library, civic center, high school, or community college. Attend a few meetings to see if this group offers the support that you need. If not, it's not difficult to form your own group. Besides, it's well worth the effort. Here are three suggestions for starting a group:

1. Recruit. Start by recruiting members through your library or school system. You can also attend local community meetings to recruit people. Parent-teacher organizations, school boards, adult education classes, and civic groups (Rotary, Lions, and so on) are often great places to meet people who are looking to improve their writing skills and learn to write creatively.

2. Set a meeting place. When you get a core group of people, it's time to find a place to meet. Most libraries rent rooms free of charge to local groups, or you may want to meet in a book-store or restaurant. Eating does distract from the serious busi-ness of critiquing writing, but it adds a delightful social atmosphere that can often build cohesiveness and keep a group running for years.

I'm not a fan of meeting in people's homes, because this makes the group more personal than professional. Also, there are often distractions in homes, such as barking dogs and ring-ing telephones. Likewise, try to avoid meeting in religious facilities because some members of different faiths might feel uncomfortable.

3. Establish guidelines. At the first few meetings, decide the following issues:

- ❦ How often to meet

- ❦ How many people to admit

- ❦ How to conduct meetings

- ❦ The purpose of the group (to encourage people to write, to help members improve their writing, to help members get published, and so on)

Running a Writers' Group

Some writers' groups are very formal, with a set procedure; others are quite casual, with a free-flowing atmosphere. The two groups to which I belong are casual, but the one I moderate has a fixed procedure. Here's how I've organized the group I moderate:

- ❦ We sit in a large circle facing each other. We don't have a large table, but I think one would be very helpful to establish a businesslike atmosphere and provide a firm writing surface. As I mentioned earlier in this chapter, members come prepared with copies of writing they want to share.

- ❦ Core members share any news about their writing, such as milestones (posting blog entries, finishing essays and stories, and so on), public readings, awards, grants, and publications.

- ❦ Any newcomers introduce themselves and briefly explain their writing interests.

- ❦ We try not to spend too much time socializing because we like to devote most of the meeting to discussing actual writing.

- ❦ Participants who want to share their work volunteer to do so. They usually read their manuscript aloud while we follow along on the copies they have made. Other times, we read the manuscript silently to ourselves. We don't let any one person monopolize the group's time by sharing an overly long piece. For example, a writer can share one chapter of a novel each meeting, but never the whole novel at once.

❧ People offer praise and mild suggestions for improvements. We write stronger suggestions, outright criticism, and any corrections in grammar and usage right on the copy we have.

❧ It's not enough to say "This didn't work for me" or "I didn't like this," because such comments aren't helpful to the writer. Instead, all criticism must be accompanied by suggestions for revision, such as "This didn't work for me because I couldn't follow the flashback. Perhaps you might want to set it off in italics."

❧ The writer may or may not respond to suggestions and offer clarification. No one is ever obligated to defend choices made as a writer.

❧ All the copies are returned to the writer for his or her review. Remember, we have written comments on them.

❧ In subsequent meetings, writers can present the same piece again and again, revised as they wish.

> When it comes to writers' groups, size matters. Groups that are too large don't give everyone time to talk, while those that are too small don't allow for enough give-and-take. Groups of six to twelve writers work well.

In the group that I moderate, the writers are mature and polite, so we've never had a problem with destructive, belittling criticism. Of course, such comments are strictly off limits, along with personal attacks and other upsetting remarks.

Live Versus Online Writers' Groups

Both live and virtual writers' groups have their strengths and weaknesses. On one hand, meeting face-to-face offers more immediate feedback. Meeting face-to-face makes it easier to clarify any confusing comments, too. Writing can be a very lonely occupation, and it's nice to get out and socialize with likeminded people.

Online writers' groups, however, are perfect if you live in an isolated area or it is difficult for you to get out of the house. Online writers' groups offer several advantages over face-to-face ones:

- ❧ If you are shy about presenting your work, you don't have to speak to people in person about it.

- ❧ If you're not sure that your critique of someone's work is on target, you are protected from embarrassment by distance and anonymity.

- ❧ You can attract people from all over the world.

- ❧ You can make far-flung connections as you network.

- ❧ You can make sure that no one is left out who wants to participate.

> You may also wish to join professional writers' organizations such as the Romance Writers of America. Professional organizations offer many advantages to creative writers, experienced as well as novice ones.

Publishing on the Internet

A few years ago the famous horror writer Stephen King shocked major publishers into jump-starting their digital book divisions when he had his publisher, Simon & Schuster, issue his novella *Riding the Bullet* in electronic form. Nearly half a million eager fans logged on to download the novella as soon as it was posted.

A few months later King bypassed Simon & Schuster completely and issued *The Plant* himself. In so doing, King became the first major author to self-publish on the Internet. Fans were instructed to send one dollar and download the first installment from his Web site, www.stephenking.com. Payment was strictly on the honor plan, and King vowed to continue the project if 75 percent of the buyers paid. To date, more than four hundred thousand people have downloaded his book.

"I have a sense of being in a place and time where I might actually make a difference in how people view the Web," King said in a *New York Times* interview. "There is a possibility of opening up an area of publishing that won't be touched by the major publishers—not necessarily for John Grisham or Tom Clancy, because they don't need to do this, but this might be a way for a lot of other writers to publish." (*New York Times,* July 24, 2000, C1)

Since King's bold move, all major publishers have increased their output of electronic books, and many have started divisions strictly devoted to electronic publishing. Their services include distributing already-existing books on the Internet as well as printing low-selling books one at a time. (This is called on-demand printing.)

An Entirely New Way to Publish?
Other writers followed King's lead with lightning speed. Seth Godin, for example, self-published his book *Unleashing the Ideavirus* on the Internet. Simon & Schuster had offered Godin a contract with an advance, but he turned it down. Instead, Godin persuaded amazon.com and Barnes&Noble.com to distribute electronic editions free to anyone who wanted to download the book.

Godin predicts that unpublished authors will offer their work online because it is an inexpensive and easy way to attract readership. Published authors will also like this publishing option, Godin believes, because it will be far more lucrative. I think online publishing is a great deal for many authors, but I can't imagine that publishers are going to jump at the chance to give a greater share of their profits to the author.

Do It Yourself E-Publishing

What does this mean for you? Thanks to Stephen King and other innovative and creative writers like him, it means that the portal to Internet self-publishing is wide open. This gives you an easy, inexpensive way to reach many people with your writing. Here are some ways that you can publish on the Internet.

- ❧ Start by establishing your own Web page. I found that the easiest way to do this was to hire a computer expert to set up my Web page. Since the expert happens to be my son, he works cheap. You can hire Web experts by contacting your local high school or college. Or you can hire a professional Web service. If you're Internet savvy, you can set up a Web page yourself by using the software that comes bundled with many computers. Many servers offer easy directions for setting up a Web page. I scanned in my picture, wrote a brief biography, and added the covers from my most popular books. I also list any upcoming writing workshops, writers' groups, and public appearances. As with writing, when it comes to a Web design, let your creativity soar!

- ❧ Rent space from a writers' organization or a server. There are a number of online writers' groups that offer free Web pages. They'll not only set up the page for you but also help you post your writing. Since more and more organizations are helping writers this way, search the Web for organizations that most closely match your interests and types of writing.

- ❧ Display part of your writing on your Web page. Displaying an excerpt entices readers to buy the rest of the book. This is ideal for self-help books and suspense novels, for example. Many big publishers are doing just that. One huge publisher reserves the right to post up to 25 percent of any book on its Web site as a marketing tool. That's fully a quarter of the manuscript! If publishers can do it, so can we—especially when we own the entire work.

❧ Display the entire document on your Web page. You can upload the entire document and have people read it online rather than being able to download it. Having your writing available in electronic form is a good way to build up a fan base, as readers will eagerly await your next endeavor. And since you're not soliciting money for your writing, you don't have to deal with the problems of mail order, an online bookseller, or King's honor system.

❧ Offer the book online and in print. You can publish your writing on your Web page and allow readers to download and print it. This is what Stephen King and Seth Godin (among others) did. You can decide whether or not to charge for the downloading.

If you choose, you can use your Web success to attract a traditional publisher to issue the book in print form later. A number of romance writers, mystery writers, and short story writers have gone this route.

Self-Publishing

In years past, paying to have your book published was considered a step down from publishing with a traditional publishing company. But now more and more writers are self-publishing. They may want to have total control over the product or are disappointed at the way a traditional publisher handled a previous book.

There are two ways you can self-publish: through so-called vanity presses or by working completely on your own through a commercial printer. Let's first see how vanity presses work.

Vanity Presses

Vanity presses offer regular publishing services, but the author pays the total cost of publishing the book. In return, the author usually receives 40 percent of the net profit and 80 percent of the subsidiary rights if the book is sold. Traditional publishers usually grant 7 to 15 percent of the net profits and 25 to 50 percent of the subsidiary rights. Figure on spending up to two thousand dollars to publish your book this way.

In the past, book reviewers didn't look kindly on books that had been issued by vanity presses. They figured that the books had been rejected by large and small publishers. As a result, writers were not likely to get any publicity at all if they published via this route. More and more, however, reviewers are taking notice of self-published books. But keep in mind that since vanity publishers make all their money up front, they have little incentive to promote your book.

Many of these businesses are advertised in the Yellow Pages under "Publishers." Before you hire one of these firms, check them out with the Better Business Bureau.

Vanity publishing may be right for you if you

1. want just a few copies of your book for family, friends, and colleagues (vanity publishing may be ideal for a memoir, for instance);
2. want total control of the project;
3. have the time to manage the project;
4. are eager to sell your book and can promote it on your own;
5. have the money to lay out for the project.

True Self-Publishing

When you self-publish, you're totally on your own. You take the manuscript to a printer or copy shop and handle marketing and distribution yourself. But you'll be in good company; self-publishers have included Zane Grey, Mark Twain, Edgar Allan Poe, Richard Nixon, James Joyce, and Carl Sandburg.

It takes a great deal of time and effort to self-publish, so think it over carefully. While the returns of publishing a book yourself can be greater than the returns from a vanity press or a large publisher, it's also time taken away from your writing. A lot of time.

Self-publish if you feel you

1. have the time and money;
2. are comfortable promoting your book on your own;
3. feel strongly about maintaining complete control of your book;
4. are eager to start and run a business (because that's what you'll be doing).

> Looking for a bit of a push to write? Join NaNoWriMo, National Novel Writing Month (held in November) and write a fifty-thousand-word novel in a month. Nearly eighty thousand people registered in 2006, and thirteen thousand finished. There are no prizes, and everyone who finishes is declared a winner. Check out their Web site at http://www.nanowrimo.org.

Publishing with a Publishing Company

Authors can also sell their manuscripts to a publishing company. The publishing company is responsible for editing, printing, and distributing the work. As the writer, you will be offered one of two different deals:

1. *Work made for hire:* In exchange for an upfront fee, the writer signs away all rights to the work. These contracts are usually offered for young adult works, nonfiction, or textbook writing.
2. *Advance and royalty:* The writer gets a percentage of future profits (an *advance*) and the promise of a percentage of any sales (a *royalty*).

Both contracts are essentially a gamble. With a work made for hire contract, you are gambling that the work won't sell, so you take the money and run. With an advance and royalty contract, you are gambling that the writing will sell, and so you'll see money in the future.

Sometimes you will have a choice of contracts; other times, you won't. In general, go for the advance and royalty deal, since it gives the publisher the greatest incentive to sell the book and recoup the advance.

Here's a summary in chart form:

Type of Contract	Advantage	Disadvantage
Work made for hire	You usually get more money upfront.	You relinquish all rights to the work.
	You are completely done with the book. You can move on to the next project.	You can't change or revise the book in any way, you rarely get copies of your work, your work may be part of a larger book.
Advance and royalty	You get a percentage of sales.	The book may not sell, so you'll get no more money.
	The publisher has an incentive to sell the book.	You may have to do publicity to promote the book.
	Since you own the work, you can resell it when the contract runs out.	You may also have to do revisions on subsequent revisions.

Stiff Competition

I'd be lying to you if I told you it was easy to get published with a large publishing company. Every year hundreds of thousands of manuscripts are submitted to publishers; they are tossed over the transom, stuffed under the mat, whizzed through the U.S. mail, and zapped through cyberspace. Some even find their way to an editor's attention. But according to www.bookwire.com, only about 120,000 brand-new novels are published every year. Most of these novels are solicited by the publishers. Only a handful come from first-time novelists. Short stories and memoirs can be even more difficult to sell. Further, a novel that's considered successful sells only 5,000 copies. A successful nonfiction book sells 7,500 copies. (Source: Authors Guild, www.authorsguild.org)

It *is* difficult to get your novel published, but it *isn't* the impossible dream. Publishers are actively looking for fresh, new writing. To publish, you need the three T's: talent, tenacity, and a tough skin. I *know* you have talent. You'll acquire tenacity and a tough skin bit by bit.

> "Write what you care about and understand. Writers should never try to outguess the marketplace in search of a salable idea; the simple truth is that all good books will eventually find a publisher if the writer tries hard enough, and a central secret to writing a good book is to write what people like you will enjoy."
> —Richard North Patterson

To increase their chances of success, the large publishers spend 80 percent of their effort on the top 20 percent of their books. If you're in the bottom 20 percent, you're going to have to beat the bushes yourself before the publisher will throw promotion money your way. Beat away; it worked for me.

Large publishers may be right for you if you

1. value this type of recognition;
2. are willing to network and make connections;
3. are content with the editorial policies and fee structure they offer.

Specialized Publishers

Specialized publishers focus on small market segments such as regional books, poetry, technical books, and so on. The largest of the small presses often publish only twenty-five or so titles a year; the smallest of the small presses are very small indeed. To find a small press, consult Dustbooks' *International Directory of Little Magazines and Small Presses* as well as *Literary Market Place*.

Although smaller publishers can be very pleasant to deal with because they can provide a personal touch, they face the same economic constraints as the big guys. They still have to reckon with the bottom line—skyrocketing paper costs and a lack of serious readers.

Specialized publishers are right for you if you

1. wrote a book on a very specific topic;
2. have targeted a niche market;
3. want to retain more control over your book.

Reference Books
You can find all the large and small publishers in the United States and Canada listed in *Literary Market Place*. This reference book, available in most libraries and online, provides the names, addresses, and publication requirements of all the major publishers. Currently, *LMP* lists more than thirty thousand publishers. *Writer's Market* is another excellent source for this information. Both of these books and their Web sites also contain the following valuable information:

Advice for making your first sale
Consumer magazines
Copyrighting information
Literary agents and agencies
Pricing guidelines
Scriptwriting information
Sections on contracts and
   agreements

Tax information
Trade, professional, and
   technical journals.
Writers' awards
Writers' contests
Your rights as a writer

According to an Authors Guild survey, the average author earns about $10,000 a year (factored into that are the top earners, such as J. K. Rowling). A beginning, low-end author makes $4,000 to $10,000 a year before expenses. Experienced, well-established midlist authors who write a book only once every year or two earn $20,000 to $40,000 before expenses. Prolific authors who publish several books a year and have been publishing for fifteen years or more earn $60,000 to $100,000. The most popular authors working regularly in media fiction earn from $80,000 to $250,000 a year. (Source: http://answers.yahoo.com/question/index?qid=20060926
164503AA0c2iQ)

Using a Literary Agent

A *literary agent* is an author's representative. An agent is your *exclusive* marketing representative, so if you hire an agent, you can no longer deal with publishers directly. A literary agent sells your writing, negotiates contracts, collects all advances and royalties due to you, and keeps track of your publishing accounts. For these services, an agent takes between 10 to 15 percent of your profits.

Assume that you're a beginning writer working on your first book. If you've created a strong synopsis for your novel and have several impressive chapters written, you might first want to publish some excerpts from your novel in mass-market magazines, literary magazines, or online to gather attention and build your platform. This will give you the foundation for a literary track record, which will encourage an agent to represent you if you decide that's what you want.

If you sell your first book on your own, you may want to have an agent close the deal. That's because a good agent can often help you get better terms than you would on your own. This paves the way for more lucrative contracts in the future, too. Only you can decide if and when you need an agent to represent you.

Finding an Agent

If you do decide you need an agent, start by consulting *Literary Market Place*, the writer's reference book described earlier in this chapter. It lists several hundred literary agencies and agents. You can also consult these sources:

❧ The Association of Authors' Representatives (www.aar-online.org)

❧ *Publishers Weekly*

❧ Genre-specific magazines (agents often advertise in genre-specific magazines)

❧ Recommendations from writers who are pleased with their agent

You Must Remember This

The writer Barbara Kingsolver said, "This manuscript of yours that has just come back from another editor is a precious package.

Don't consider it rejected. Consider that you've addressed it 'to the editor who can appreciate my work' and it has simply come back stamped 'Not at this address.' Just keep looking for the right address."

You have the write stuff. Believe in yourself—and write on!

CHAPTER 12
Reviewing Writing Skills

———— ≈≈≈ ————

Dangling participles. Double negatives. Demonstrative pronouns. What *do* these terms mean? When most people say they can't write, they're often referring to problems with grammar and usage. If you're unsure about grammar, usage, and other writing skills, it's time to relax. In this chapter, you'll review all the basics in detail. Then you'll be ready to concentrate on expressing yourself freely in writing.

To make the most of your time, read this chapter all the way through. As you read, keep a list of the grammar and usage rules that you find most confusing. Focus on learning those specific rules rather than trying to master all the rules of grammar and usage at once. You'll remember more if you focus on your individual writing problems.

Let's focus on the top skill problems that plague creative writers. I've arranged the rules in alphabetical order to make it easier for you to read them the first time and then refer back to them as necessary.

If you feel yourself getting overwhelmed by all this grammar and usage, remember that Shakespeare bent all the rules (he even spelled his own name a dozen different ways), and it didn't stand in the way of his writing one bit!

Adjectives
Adjectives describe nouns and pronouns. Adjectives answer the questions *What kind? How much? Which one?* or *How many?*

There are four kinds of adjectives: *articles, common adjectives, compound adjectives,* and *proper adjectives.*

Articles: A, an, and *the* are articles.
The is called the definite article because it refers to a specific thing.
Examples: *The* blog   *The* short story   *The* book

A and *an* are indefinite articles because they refer to general things.
Examples: *A* blog   *A* short story   *An* author

Use *an* in place of *a* when it precedes a vowel sound, not just a vowel.
Examples: *an* honor   *a* UFO

> Second-language speakers find definite and indefinite articles very challenging, because the rules are often entirely arbitrary—why are you *in* town but *in the* city?

Common Adjectives: Describe nouns or pronouns.
Examples: *thick* manuscript   *superb* story   *wonderful* novel

Compound Adjectives: Are made up of more than one word.
Examples: *fifteen-minute* presentation   *black-and-blue* mark

Proper Adjectives: Are formed from proper nouns.
Examples: *Spanish* rice   *Shakespearean* English

Here are two suggestions for using adjectives skillfully:
1. Use an adjective to describe a noun or a pronoun.
2. Choose precise adjectives rather than using a string of them. One perfect adjective is far more powerful than a string of vague or imprecise ones.

Adverbs

Adverbs describe verbs, adjectives, or other adverbs. Adverbs answer the questions: *When? Where? How?* or *To What Extent?*

Most adverbs are formed by adding -*ly* to an adjective.

Examples: ate *hurriedly*   walked *leisurely*   sat *watchfully*

Common Adverbs That *Don't* End in -*ly*

afterward	almost	already	also
back	even	far	fast
hard	here	how	late
long	low	more	never
next	now	often	rather
so	soon	still	then
there	today	too	tomorrow
when	where	yesterday	

Here are two suggestions for using adverbs skillfully:

1. Use an adverb to describe a verb, an adjective, or another adverb.
2. As with adjectives, choose the precise adverb to get just the meaning you want. You can use an online or print thesaurus to help you find appropriate adjectives and adverbs.

Comparing with Adjectives and Adverbs

Adjectives and adverbs are often used to compare by showing that one thing is larger, smaller, bigger, or more important than something else. Adjectives and adverbs are called *modifiers* because they modify or change other words. English makes this easy by giving us a special way to compare two things (the *comparative degree*) and a special way to compare more than two things (the *superlative degree*). Here's how to do it:

> *Comparative Degree:* Use the *comparative degree* (-*er* or *more* form) to compare two things. Use –*er* with most one- and two-syllable modifiers; use *more* with most three-syllable modifiers.
>
> Examples: Micha is *smarter* than Nanci.
>
> Henri is *more affectionate* than Tasha.

Superlative Degree: Use the *superlative degree* (-*est* or *most* form) to compare more than two things. Use -*est* with most one- and two-syllable modifiers; use *most* with most three-syllable modifiers.

Examples: This is the *funniest* movie I have ever seen!
Luc is the *most considerate* man in the room.

Never use -*er* and *more* or -*est* and *most* together.

Examples: **Not** I have a *more newer* car, **but** I have a *newer* car.
Not I have the *most biggest* phone bill, **but** I have the *biggest* phone bill.

Good and *bad* do not follow these guidelines. They have irregular forms, as follows:

Part of Speech	Positive	Comparative	Superlative
adjective	good	better	best
adverb	well	better	best
adjective	bad	worse	worst
adverb	badly	worse	worst

Agreement

Agreement means matching parts of a sentence. When sentence parts match, your writing sounds smooth. If they don't match, it sounds jarring or awkward.

Agreement of Pronoun and Antecedent

Pronouns and antecedents (the words to which they refer) must *agree,* or match. A personal pronoun must agree with its antecedent in number, person, and gender.

- *Number* is amount: singular or plural
- *Person* refers to first person, second person, or third person (the person speaking, the person spoken to, or the person spoken about)
- *Gender* refers to masculine, feminine, or neuter references. *He* and *him* are masculine in gender, *she* and *her* are feminine, and *it* and *its* are neutral.

Examples:

Number: *Meish and Chaya* took *their* friends to a Broadway show.
          plural subject   plural pronoun

Person: *Janice* exercised on *her* bicycle every morning.
       third person   third person

Gender: *Tony* teaches literature, a subject *he* studied in graduate school.
      masculine noun   masculine pronoun

In the past, the pronouns *he* and *his* were used to refer to both men and women. We would write or say: "A doctor should use *his* skills to help mankind," or "Everyone can learn to write well if *he* applies *himself*."

Today, using the pronouns *he* and *his* to refer to both men and women is considered sexist language. As a result, avoid this usage. Try these ideas:

- ❧ Rewrite the sentence into the third-person *they* or *them*.
  Examples: *Doctors* should use *their* skills to help humanity.
  (Notice that the sexist *mankind* has become the inclusive *humanity*.)
  People can learn to write well if *they* apply *themselves*.

- ❧ Rewrite the sentence into the second person *you*.
  Example: *You* should use *your* skills to help humanity.

- ❧ Eliminate the pronoun altogether.
  Example: Try writing different kinds of poetry.

> A pronoun replaces a noun. To make sure that your writing is clear, always use the noun first before using the pronoun.
> Example: *Jillian* sent her latest blog to her friends. *She* didn't finish writing it until 2:00 in the morning.

Agreement of Subject and Verb

To make your writing sound polished, be sure that subjects and verbs are in the same form. Here are some guidelines:

❧ A singular subject takes a singular verb.

> Example: *Nick proofreads* (not *proofread*) everything before he
>   singular singular
>   subject   verb
>
> shares it with anyone.

❧ A plural subject takes a plural verb.

> Example: *Jamal and Krystle proofread* (not *proofreads*) everything
> they write.   plural   plural
>   subject   verb

❧ Prepositional phrases that come between the subject and the verb don't affect agreement.

> Example: Too many *mistakes in an essay* can *block* meaning.
>   plural   prep.   plural
>   subject phrase   verb

(The plural subject *mistakes* requires the plural verb *block*. Ignore the prepositional phrase *in an essay*.)

❧ Subjects that are singular in meaning but plural in form take a singular verb. These subjects include words such as *measles, news,* and *economics*.

> Example: The *news was* intriguing.
>   singular singular
>   subject verb

❧ Singular subjects connected by *either/or, neither/nor,* and *not only/but also* take a singular verb.

> Example: Neither Ralph *nor* his wife *was* going to proofread the
> letter.   singular   singular
>   subject   verb

❧ If the subject is made up of two or more nouns or pronouns connected by *or, nor, not only,* or *but also,* the verb agrees with the noun closest to the pronoun.

> Examples: Neither Ralph nor the *proofreaders are* finished working.
>   plural   plural
>   subject   verb

> Neither the proofreaders nor *Ralph is* finished working.
>   singular singular
>   subject verb

Biased Language

Avoid *biased language,* words and phrases that assign qualities to people on the basis of their gender, race, religion, or health. Here are some guidelines:

❧ Avoid using *he* to refer to both men and women.
❧ Avoid using *man* to refer to both men and women.
❧ Avoid language that denigrates people.

Capitalization

Capitalization is one of the writer's most useful tools, because it helps convey meaning. For example, when readers see a capital letter, they know they've reached the beginning of a sentence, a quotation, or a person's name. This helps your audience read your writing the way you intended it to be read. Below are the rules for using capital letters correctly.

❧ Capitalize the first word of a sentence, the greeting of a letter, the complimentary close of a letter, and each item in an outline.

   Examples: This is the winter of our discontent.
   Dear John,
   Very truly yours,
   I. Introduction
   II. First main point
   III. Second main point

❧ Capitalize geographical places and sections of the country; the names of historical events, eras, and documents; and abbreviations that appear after a person's name.

   Examples: the East
   the Civil War
   the Renaissance
   the Declaration of Independence
   Maura J. Smyth, Ph.D.

❧ Capitalize the names of languages, nationalities, and races.

   Examples: German, French, Spanish
   Romanian, Swedish
   African American

❧ Capitalize proper nouns, proper adjectives, and brand names.
    Examples: Ernest Hemingway
              Italian bread
              Xerox

❧ Capitalize the names of organizations, institutions, courses, and famous buildings.
    Examples: Girl Scouts of the USA
              Museum of Natural History
              English 110, Mathematics 201 (but mathematics)
              Sears Tower

❧ Capitalize days, months, and holidays.
    Examples: Monday, Tuesday, Wednesday
              March, April, May
              Thanksgiving, Memorial Day

❧ Capitalize abbreviations for time.
    Examples: A.M., P.M.

Conjunctions

Conjunctions are words or pairs of words that link ideas. Use them to help create meaning and logic in writing. As you write, select the conjunctions that give you the precise shade of meaning you want. You may wish to choose conjunctions from this list as you write:

Conjunctions			
after	although	and	as
as if	because	before	both, and
but	either, or	even though	for
if	neither, nor	or	not only, but also
nor	since	so	so that
than	though	unless	until
when	where	wherever	while

Contractions

Contractions are two words combined into one. When you contract words, add an apostrophe in the space where the letter or letters have been taken out.

Examples:

I	+	am	=	I'm	she	+	is	=	she's
you	+	are	=	you're	we	+	are	=	we're
he	+	is	=	he's	it	+	is	=	it's

Contractions are often confused with *possessive pronouns.* Use this chart to keep the two clear:

Contraction	Possessive Pronoun
it's (it is)	its
you're (you are)	your
they're (they are)	their
who's (who is)	whose

Double Negatives

Use only one negative word to express a negative idea. Using two negative words cancels them both out.

Example: **Not** I *don't* have *no* ideas, **but** I *don't* have any ideas.

The most common negative words are *no, nobody, not, no one, nothing, nowhere, never, neither* and contractions ending in *n't (don't,* et cetera*)*.

Interjections

Interjections are words that show strong emotion. Often interjections will be set off with an exclamation mark. For example: *Watch out!, Oh!, Wow!*

Nonstandard English

Nonstandard English consists of words and phrases that are not considered standard written English.

Examples:	*Nonstandard:*	irregardless	being that	hisself
	Standard:	regardless	since	himself

However, nonstandard English can work beautifully in dialogue, as Mark Twain showed in *The Adventures of Huckleberry Finn*. Here's how the novel opens:

> *YOU don't know about me without you have read a book by the name of The Adventures of Tom Sawyer; but that ain't no matter. That book was made by Mr. Mark Twain, and he told the truth, mainly. There was things which he stretched, but mainly he told the truth. That is nothing. I never seen anybody but lied one time or another, without it was Aunt Polly, or the widow, or maybe Mary. Aunt Polly—Tom's Aunt Polly, she is—and Mary, and the Widow Douglas is all told about in that book, which is mostly a true book, with some stretchers, as I said before.*

Nouns

A *noun* is a word that names a person, place, or thing. There are different kinds of nouns, as follows:

Common nouns name a type of person, place, or thing.
Examples: play   poem   movie

Proper nouns name a specific person, place, or thing.
Examples: *King Lear*   "Mending Wall"   *Gone With the Wind*

Plural Nouns name more than one person, place, or thing. Here are the guidelines for forming plural nouns:

❧ Add *s* to form the plural of most nouns.
Examples: paper/papers   pencil/pencils   blog/blogs

❧ Add *es* if the noun ends in *s, sh, ch*, or *x*.
Examples: inch/inches   box/boxes

❧ If the noun ends in *y* preceded by a *consonant*, change the *y* to *i* and add *es*.
Examples: city/cities   baby/babies

🪶 If the noun ends in *y* preceded by a *vowel*, add *s*.

    Examples: essay/essays   journey/journeys

🪶 If the noun ends in *o* preceded by a *consonant*, some nouns take *es*, some take *s*, some take either *s* or *es*.

    Examples: hero/heroes piano/pianos motto/mottos, mottoes

🪶 Some nouns ending in *f* take *s*; others change the *f* or *fe* to *v* and add *es*

    Examples: belief/beliefs   life/lives

🪶 Some nouns change their spelling when they become plural.

    Examples: mouse/mice   foot/feet

🪶 Some nouns have the same form whether they are singular or plural.

    Examples: series   moose   species

> Use a dictionary to clarify any confusion.

Possessive Nouns
Possession shows ownership. Here's how to show possessive nouns.

🪶 Add an apostrophe and an *s* to singular nouns.

    Example: author   author's blog

🪶 With plural nouns ending in *s*, add an apostrophe after the *s*.

    Example: authors   authors' blogs

🪶 With plural nouns not ending in *s*, add an apostrophe and an *s*.

    Example: mice   mice's tails

> Remember that possessive pronouns don't require an apostrophe. The possessive pronouns are *yours, hers, its, ours, theirs,* and *whose.*

Prepositions

Prepositions are words that link a noun or a pronoun to another word in the sentence. Prepositions are useful because they allow you to show how parts of a sentence are related to each other.

Examples:　about　　off　　near　　over　　for
　　　　　　below　　in　　under　　by　　to

Pronouns

Pronouns are words used in place of a noun or another pronoun. There are several different kinds of pronouns. The most common ones are *personal pronouns, possessive pronouns, interrogative pronouns,* and *indefinite pronouns.*

Personal pronouns point out a specific person, place, object, or thing:

	Singular	*Plural*
first person	I, me, mine, my	we, us, our, ours
second person	you, your, yours	you, your, yours
third person	he, him, his, she, her, hers, it	they, them, their, theirs, its

Possessive pronouns show ownership.

Examples:　mine　yours　his　hers
　　　　　　its　　ours　theirs　whose

Interrogative pronouns begin a question.

Examples:　who　what　which　whom　whose

Indefinite pronouns refer to people, places, objects, or things without pointing to a specific one.

Examples:　another　anybody　everyone　everything
　　　　　　nobody　none　one　some

Pronoun Case

Case is the form of a noun or pronoun that shows how it is used in a sentence. English has three cases: *nominative, objective,* and *possessive.* This means that the pronouns have one form as a subject, another as an object, and a third to show possession, as the following chart shows.

Pronoun Case

Nominative (as a subject)	*Objective* (as an object)	*Possessive* (to show ownership)
I	me	my, mine
you	you	you
he	him	his
she	her	hers
it	it	its
we	us	our, ours
they	them	their, theirs
who	whom	whose
whoever	whomever	whosoever

Here are some guidelines to make it easier for you to use pronouns:

❧ Use the nominative case to show the subject of a verb. This shows who is doing the action.

Example: *I* plan to write for half an hour every day.

❧ Use the objective case to show the noun or pronoun that receives the action.

Example: The famous writer was willing to speak to *me*.

❧ Use the possessive case to show ownership.

Example: The writer gave me *his* advice about publishing.

Punctuation

Punctuation is an important writing tool because it helps determine meaning. Each mark of punctuation provides important visual clues to readers, showing where sentences begin and end, telling readers where to pause, and so on. Here are the basic rules.

Apostrophes. The (') can be used two ways:

1. To show possession (ownership)

Examples: Twain's novel   Shakespeare's play   Charles's letter

2. To show contractions (where a letter or number has been omitted).

Examples: can't   won't   didn't
           the '60s   the '90s

Brackets: Use [ ] to show words that interrupt a direct quotation.

Example: "Four score and seven years [eighty-seven years]
           ago, our fathers brought forth on this continent,
           a new nation, conceived in Liberty, and dedicated
           to the proposition that all men are created equal."

You probably won't be using brackets a lot, since it's not often that you'll have to interrupt a direct quotation to clarify or add information.

Colons: Use a colon before a list. This is a colon :

Example: Ray packed the following food for the camping
           trip: meat, granola bars, fruit, vegetables, and
           coffee.

Commas: Use a comma after introductory words and expressions, to separate items in a series, to set off interrupting words and expressions, to separate parts of a compound sentence, and in the close of any letter.

Examples:

If you want to be a creative writer, you *can* be a creative writer.
Introductory subordinate clause

You might write *a blog, a novel, a play, a journal, or an essay.*
Separating items in a series

This time, *at last,* you'll get your ideas down on paper.
Interrupting words

The important question is not when people start *writing, but* that they *do* write.
Separate parts of a compound sentence

Can't tell if you're using too many commas? When in doubt, leave the comma out.

Dashes: Use a dash to show a sudden change of thought. A dash is two hyphens, like this —

> Example: Most people can become creative writers—if they set to work.

Ellipses: Use these three spaced periods to show that something has been left out.

> Example:
> (original quote) But in a larger sense, we cannot dedicate—we cannot consecrate—we cannot hallow—this ground.
>
> (edited quote) But in a larger sense, we cannot dedicate . . . this ground.

Exclamation marks: Use an exclamation mark to show strong emotion.

> Example: I can't believe I finished writing a whole chapter of my novel!

> Unless you're writing comic books, use only one exclamation mark at the end of a sentence.

Hyphen: Use a hyphen to show a word break at the end of a line, in some compound nouns, and in fractions and in compound numbers. A hyphen is -

> Examples: great-grandfather   two-thirds   sixty-six

Parentheses: Use parentheses to enclose additional information.

> Example: Perhaps the best part about creative writing (despite the hard work) is the deep satisfaction it gives you to express your thoughts on paper.

Periods: Use a period after a declarative sentence (the end of a statement of fact or opinion) and after most abbreviations. Only use one period if an abbreviation ends a sentence.

> Examples: Many people start writing late in life.
> Some people write before work, around 7:00 A.M., while others like to write after work, around 9:00 P.M.

Question Marks: Use a question mark after a question.

    Example: Do you prefer to write in longhand or on a computer?

Quotation Marks: Use quotation marks to set off a speaker's exact words.

    Examples: "This story is good," Anne said.
                    Anne said, "This story is good."
                    "This story," Anne said, "is good."

Semicolons: Use a semicolon between main clauses when the conjunction (*and, but, for, or, yet*) has been left out, and to separate items in a series when the items contain commas.

    Examples: People write stories about topics that interest them, and they write about things that concern them.

                    People write stories about topics that interest them; they write about things that concern them.

                    I write about people, places, and ideas; and I write about social issues, including education, volunteerism, and people who have talent they are afraid to express.

Sentence Errors

A *sentence* is a group of words that expresses a complete thought. A sentence has two parts: a *subject* and a *predicate*. The subject includes the noun or pronoun that identifies the subject. The predicate contains the verb that describes what the subject is doing.

    Example: Anne Tyler   writes   novels and short stories.
                  subject   verb   predicate

Sentence Fragments and Run-Ons

Sentence *fragments* and *run-ons* are often used in dialogue to show everyday speech, but they are considered sentence errors when used in straight text.

❧ A *sentence fragment* is a group of words that does not express a complete thought. It may also be missing a subject, verb, or both.

Example: Wrote all night.   *I* wrote all night.

❧ A *run-on sentence* consists of two incorrectly joined sentences.

Example: It's important for writers to get feedback everyone one needs an editor.

There are three ways to correct a run-on sentence:

1. Separate the run-on into two sentences:
   Example: It's important for writers to get feedback.
   Everyone needs an editor.

2. Add a conjunction. You might add a coordinating conjunction (*and, but, or, for, yet, so*).
   Example: It's important for writers to get feedback, for everyone needs an editor.

   You might add a subordinating conjunction.
   Example: It's important for writers to get feedback, because everyone needs an editor.

3. Add a semicolon.
   Example: It's important for writers to get feedback; everyone needs an editor.

Select the repair method depending on your audience, purpose, and unique writing style.

Dangling Modifiers

A *dangling modifier* is a word or phrase that describes something that has been left out of the sentence. As a result, the sentence does not convey the correct meaning. It may also unintentionally cause humor. Correct a dangling modifier by adding a noun or pronoun to which the dangling modifier can be attached.

Example: *Dangling:* Coming up the stairs, the clock struck midnight.

Correct: As he was coming up the stairs, the clock struck midnight.

Misplaced Modifiers

A *misplaced modifier* is a descriptive word or phrase that is placed too far away from the noun or the pronoun that it describes. As a result, the sentence is unclear. It may be confusing or unintentionally funny. To correct a misplaced modifier, move the modifier as close as possible to the word or phrase it is describing, as the following example shows:

Example: *Misplaced:* We bought a puppy for my brother we call Fido.

Correct: We bought a puppy we call Fido for my brother.

Transitions

Transitions—words and expressions that signal connections among ideas—can help you achieve coherence in your writing. Each transition signals to the reader how one idea is connected to the next. You'll want to choose the transitions that link your ideas just the way you want. You can use the following chart to help you make your choices:

Transitions	Relationship
and, also, besides, in addition to, too	Addition
thus, namely, for instance, for example	Example
next, then, finally, second (third, fourth, etc.), before, soon, afterwards, during, later, meanwhile	Time

but, still, yet, if, however, nevertheless, in contrast	Contrast
likewise, similarly, here, in comparison	Comparison
in the front, in the back, there, nearby	Location
therefore, thus, consequently, as a result, due to this, accordingly	Result
as a result, in brief, hence, in short, finally, in conclusion	Summary

Verbs

Verbs are words that name an action or describe a state of being. There are three types of verbs: *action verbs, linking verbs, helping verbs.*

Action verbs tell what the subject does.

Examples: dance   frolic   stroll   nap

Linking verbs join the subject and the predicate and name and describe the subject.

Examples:
appear	be	become	feel
grow	look	remain	seem
smell	sound	stay	taste
turn			

Helping verbs are added to another verb to make the meaning clearer.

Examples:
am	can	could	does
had	might	will	would

While all three types of verbs are necessary in writing, action verbs make your writing forceful while linking verbs tend to make it wordy. As a result, you'll probably want to use action verbs whenever possible.

Verb Tense and Voice

Verbs can show time, called *tense*. Avoid shifting tenses in the middle of a sentence or a paragraph because it confuses readers.

Examples: **Not** I *walked* to the park and I *feed* the birds,
    past   present
    tense   tense

      but I *walked* to the park and I *fed* the birds.
    past   past
    tense   tense

In addition to showing time, most verbs also indicate whether the subject is performing an action or having an action performed on it. This is called verb *voice*. English has two verb voices: the *active voice* and the *passive voice*.

❧ In the active voice, the subject performs the action.
   Example: Marissa bought a bag of potatoes.

❧ In the passive voice, the action is performed upon the subject.
   Example: The bag of potatoes was bought by Marissa.

The active voice is usually preferable to the passive because it is more vigorous and concise. For example, notice that there are eight words in the second example, but only six words in the first. Who needs that *was* or *by*? These words don't add anything to the meaning; in fact, they make the sentence wordy.

However, use the passive voice to avoid placing blame or when you don't know who performed the action.
   Examples: A problem occurred.   A door was left ajar.

You Must Remember This

Grammar and *usage* are the customary ways we use language in speech and writing. *Punctuation* is the use of standard marks in written language to clarify meaning. Make the rules your own by using them to convey your precise meaning.

Acknowledgments

A book is never produced by one person alone, despite what it says on the front page! My deepest thanks to all the people at Madison Park Press who make me look so good: executive editor Christine Zika, production editor Lisa Thornbloom, designer Christos Peterson, and editorial assistant Jennifer Puglisi. You are all dedicated, professional, and tremendously talented.